SMALL TOWN Sexy

the allure of living in small town America

KIM HUSTON

The
Clark
Group

Lexington, Kentucky

Clark Publishing
dba The Clark Group
250 East Short Street
Lexington, KY 40507
800 944 3995   info@theclarkgroupinfo.com

Visit our Web site at www.TheClarkGroupInfo.com

First Edition: August 2009

Printed in the United States of America.
10 9 8 7 6 5 4 3 2 1

ISBN: 978-0-9822201-4-6 soft cover edition
ISBN: 978-0-9822201-7-7 hard cover edition

Cover design by Ginny Roby Holland
Illustrations by Tom Ballard
Book design by Kelly Elliott

DEDICATION

To my parents—
who allowed me a wonderfully grounded childhood
in small town America
and encouraged the thought
that a small town is only small by population
but is enormous
in spirit.
And to my brother—
who shared this life with me.

Contents

ACKNOWLEDGEMENTS

I love watching *The Academy Awards*. I love the glitz and glamour of Hollywood, the beautiful people and the even more amazing fashion statements. I love sitting on the edge of my seat waiting for them to announce the winners, keeping my fingers crossed for my favorite actors and or movie. What I dread, however, are those lengthy Academy Award winning speeches. You know the ones, where they always have to list everyone and their brother after receiving their Oscar. Why is it important to thank so many people? The actors seem to ramble on forever, until the music starts to play, which is their cue to wrap it up. Why?

After months of writing this book, I finally know why.

It is because no one truly does it alone. Behind every successful actor, every successful movie, there are numerous others who had their hand in making this success possible. Whether it's an acting coach, a life coach, a fellow actor or a relative, we may not ever know them or see them, but they have been there when it has been important in this person's career. It is that perfect time to thank that person who helped get you to where you are today.

So with that said, and knowing that chances of me ever giving an Academy Award speech are pretty slim, I am going to give you what my speech would be, if they gave an Oscar for the best in *Small Town Sexy* books:

Small Town Sexy has been an incredible journey where some of my most vivid childhood memories have come to life in the pages of this book. It was born from a lifetime of my own memories and those of many small town enthusiasts just like me who unconditionally shared their stories in some very colorful ways.

I write from the heart. I don't consider myself a great story teller— I just tell things as I see them. So that combination, and a lot of good friends cheering me along the way, made this sometimes painful process a whole lot of fun. (Despite the neck aches and the gaining of five pounds while sitting and writing each evening.)

First, and foremost, I must thank Bobby Clark, my publisher and my biggest cheerleader along the way. He saw an idea, believed in me and convinced me it could be a book. He was right—as he was throughout this entire process—and I thank him for his professional persistence along this journey. More importantly, Bobby is now a good friend.

Paul Sanders, my writing mentor and editor, who knew my voice better than I did. He was there as I would lose my way, always to bring me back to an even better, more creative place. He was my focus to keep it real and inspired me to as he put it, "Be the one who sings the solo for this small town chorus." You are an amazing soul.

Tim Ballard, the smartest person I know and who also shares my small town heritage. Your support at the end of this project made me realize that this is a story that needed to be told and I am glad you were there to help make that happen. Although not related by blood, you will always be family.

Kim Rogers, my assistant at my "real" job, who was always more excited than me about this project and who gave priceless feedback throughout the journey.

Ginny Roby Holland, my art designer, who has an eye for style. She made small town "sexy" with her creative sense of flair.

Tom Ballard, who has been a constant friend, always there to tell me the honest truth whether I wanted to hear it or not. An artist, photographer and illustrator, he knows how to make me and any project I undertake, look good.

Sandy Romenesko, my Mt. Sterling, Kentucky counterpart in economic development, and who is the epitome of *Small Town Sexy*. Her funny small town stories inspired me to realize that there was a book that needed to be written.

Julie Wilson Garrett and Jane Roby, my "Sunshine Girls" who were my cheerleaders from start to finish, and who, over many glasses of wine, inspired my many chapter titles and contents.

Alice and Dick Heaton, whose lifelong love and appreciation of small town life are evidenced by the passion they have for their hometown of Bardstown, Kentucky.

To my small town friends, now living the big city life, who shared with me their beautifully written childhood stories. Sammy Beam, my childhood ventriloquist partner—now a Hollywood decorative artist and designer—who has an unbelievable sense of style in anything he does. And Ned Johnson, my former radio co-host, who as a college English professor in Tampa, Florida, lived his own Mayberry and can tell a story better than Mark Twain.

To my Facebook friends, my LinkedIn connections, my followers on Twitter, and website Bloggers, thank you for telling me your small town stories and for your storyline suggestions.

To those I interviewed for the book and who gave their time to answer dozens of questions, thank you for your patience and for your insight into small town life. To those lucky enough to live in any of the small towns mentioned in the book—you are a member of a fortunate "small town society." Be thankful for where you wake up each morning.

And I have saved my best for last.

My daughters Erin and Meg, who keep me young and energetic but don't let me dress too young for my age. Despite the fact that this project took a bit of time away from "our" time, their love and patience kept me going. I kept their Mother's Day card on my desk as daily inspiration. It reads "Mom, you've always been there, cheering me on, loving me for who I am and who I can be. You're simply one of the most important people in my life." Well girls, I couldn't have written my feelings for you any better, so back 'atcha! A bit of mother's advice to you, keep a journal and write! You will be glad you did in about twenty years.

And finally, to Mike, who is my daily dose of reality and sensibility. Thank you for listening to my whining when writer's block set in, rubbing my neck after sitting in front of the computer for hours, and for making me walk away from the computer late at night when I could no longer spell the word "sexy." I am honored to share my life with you and look forward to making many new small town memories together. After this project, that mountain we have talked about climbing will seem like a breeze. Get the backpacks out. I am ready when you are. Love you—mean it!

And, finally I would like to thank the *Small Town Sexy* Academy for making this possible.

"The nice part about living in a small town,

is that when you don't know what you're doing,

someone else does."

—Author unknown

What's Love Got To Do With It?

ow do I even begin to describe it?

It started as just a simple relationship; we were young and very vulnerable. It was a genuine mutual attraction. For years we were together, day after day, when I laughed and when tears would roll down my cheeks. We were only apart for brief periods of time, and I was always anxious to return. This relationship matured, as did I, and this crush turned to the kind of feeling that you get deep inside—and you know you have to have a little more. It was not a feeling that I could hide, though at times, I felt it necessary to do so, knowing my friends would not understand. The longer I was away, the stronger my feelings became. There was a true fireworks-bursting, over-the-fence, out-of-the-park kind of feeling every time I returned. Not even the distance that I put between us would make this feeling go away.

I was almost embarrassed and ashamed to admit to it to my friends, but I knew I had to because the rest of my life would depend on how I would handle this secret. I finally had to confess my feelings. I was twenty-two years old when I sat down with my closest friends over a glass of wine and told them . . .

I couldn't stay away any longer because I needed to be where my heart was. I was moving back to what I missed and loved most—I was going home to small town America.

Okay, I know some of you may be saying to yourself right now "What the heck?" Who falls in love with their town? What's with that?

But believe me, as odd as it may sound to you, it is true and it's a feeling that I can only associate with a long-time love affair.

It was encouraging to learn while writing this book that I was not alone. During my research, I learned there are many out there with this same love of community, just not wanting to come out of the closet with this feeling, and certainly not willing to express it in such ridiculously colorful terms.

I want to build no pretense between us; I have to be honest before you read any further. If you just sat down, wide-eyed and looking forward to reading about scandalous love affairs and sex in small town America, a small town "tell-all" book—you will be sadly disappointed. I can assure you that small towns do have their share of scandals and sex. Not unlike my favorite big city characters in *Sex in the City*, women in small towns do sit around and talk about their love lives, their sex lives, and the even the lives of everyone around them. These conversations may not take place in fancy bars, but our late night bunko parties or margarita night at the Mexican restaurants can be considered the small town equivalents.

I am pretty confident that if I asked you to write down five things you associate with being "sexy" that "small towns" would probably not make your list and understandably so. We tend to associate sexy with people, like Victoria Secret models, or places like beaches, and anywhere tropical and sunny. Big cities may make your sexy list because of the bright lights and the endless things to do after dark.

However, for this book, the word "sexy" in the title has a bit of a different meaning.

This book is about passion—the passion and infatuation that so many people have for small towns and their lives and adventures there. I have a story to tell. So throughout this book you will get to know me and read about the small town experiences that I have had over the decades and realize how much I cherish my roots as a small town girl.

But more importantly, *Small Town Sexy* is filled with stories (I swear, I couldn't make this stuff up), opinions and anecdotes from some of the smartest and wisest people I know, who have spent their lives promoting life in small town America. I have even called in favors from my "big city" friends who give a balance to many of our stories.

And finally, the book contains many excerpts from my new cyber-friends I met along the way—who found my website and posted their Blogs, added me as a friend on Facebook, a connection on LinkedIn and followed me on Twitter. All these social networking resources available today make it possible to get a national overview of life in small towns from those who experience it every day and who believe that small towns are in fact a sexy place to live.

*O*kay, so you are asking yourself, how can you honestly put the words "small town" and "sexy" in the same sentence or as a title to a book? It's kind of like putting the words "puppy" and "frightening" together—they just don't fit. Right? Well, it's quite simple. The word "sexy" in my title refers to the allure and the appeal of living in small town America and the seductive charm that so many of these towns have that causes their residents to never want to leave. Sexy means interesting, engaging, pleasing and fascinating—all things that are the essence of small towns. So many small towns exude a certain charisma and charm that pull residents in and won't let them go. The "sexy" in *Small Town Sexy* also refers to the self-assurance that small town residents have in where they live and the quality of their lives there. In their minds they are living big in a small town and nothing is unattainable. That attitude exudes *Small Town Sexy*.

I fell for that seductive small town charm the moment I was old enough to get a sense of where I lived.

My parents, both of whom were products of small towns, are actually the ones who deserve the credit for my desire to remain there. They kept me grounded with idyllic small town activities, like participating in Vacation Bible School, sleigh rides during the winter, pot luck suppers in the fall, organizing yard sales and riding the back roads on a Sunday afternoon in our station wagon. My life growing up was a wonderful yet simple life, and one that I have tried to imitate with my own daughters, Erin and Meg. I hope I have left an imprint of small town passion with them; however, they are adventurous spirits who I am sure will want to explore many new places before considering life in their hometown.

And now, as I continue to live my life in a sexy small town, it has become apparent that I am not alone in this crazy love affair. It is a contagious way of life that so many people are choosing and if you are lucky, you too, will have the chance to experience all the goodness a small town has to offer.

What is it about this small town charm that continues to seduce newcomers? What is it about this way of life that has so many people and their families once again, coming back to the country?

And the essential question remains, WHAT IS SEXY ABOUT LIVING IN A SMALL TOWN?

Over the following chapters, I hope to seduce your mind with some wonderful small town stories, so that you too will "get it" and be able to answer that question emphatically.

*I*n a small town we . . .

. . . walk with a smile for no apparent reason
. . . give directions by landmarks rather than mileage or street names
. . . still sell Girl Scout cookies door to door
. . . still believe that county fairs are the highlight of the summer
. . . mourn the loss of a company or industry
. . . keep our doors unlocked so our repairmen can come and fix things
. . . enjoy chili suppers at the hospital auxiliary, fish fries at the American
    Legion, bake sales at the church, and lemonade stands still line our
    streets during the summers
. . . can still order cherry Coke from our downtown soda fountains
. . . have generations of families in leadership positions
. . . have those same generations of families living in the same houses
. . . pull over when a funeral procession goes by
. . . can still charge things at the local hardware store
. . . can buy produce straight from the farm at our farmers markets
. . . are taught by teachers who taught our parents
. . . dial a wrong number and know the person on the misdialed call
. . . can entertain ourselves on our front porches rather than in front of
    our TVs

"A small town is a place
there's no place to go where you shouldn't."
—*Burt Bacharach*

chapter one

ONE SIZE DOESN'T FIT ALL

*W*hat is sexy about living in a small town?"

If you were to visit ten different small towns and ask ten different people in those towns, chances are you would get over fifty different answers to the question:

Is it the slower pace?

Is it the quality of life?

Is it the cost of living?

According to my research, the answer is yes, yes and yes again. All of these play an enormous role in making a *Small Town Sexy*. And if you're saying to yourself, "A small town is just another town." What's the deal? Well, I have to tell you—that's like saying Tiger Woods is just another golfer.

*B*efore we go much further we probably need to quantify what population range we define as a small town and the labels we use to describe it. There are many terms that people use today to describe a small town and the surrounding area, including town, community, village, hamlet, rural, country, Hicksville, and Podunk Junction (well, maybe not those last two though I do find them funny). During this book I will probably use each of these words, more than once, as they relate to various stories being told about different types of small towns.

Now, let's talk size. I am proud to say that in this book, size DOES NOT matter! Okay, for those of you who took that comment inappropriately, go ahead and giggle for a second. Now, slap your hand and get your mind back on small towns, because you are going to hear that reference a lot. This book will emphasize that less is best and small things rule.

The National League of Cities reports that eighty-seven percent of cities listed in the 2000 census have ten thousand residents or less. They go on to say that these cities "are more representative of cities nationwide."

The research also shows that small cities under ten thousand grew considerably faster (18.5 percent) than large and medium sized cities during the 1990s. We have also learned that small cities within metropolitan areas are growing at faster rates than small cities outside a metro area.

Apparently being born in a small town is a great prerequisite for someone who spends most of her waking hours being a nationally recognized champion of community. Sylvia Lovely, president of the NewCities Institute, was born in the small town of Frenchburg, Kentucky (Pop. 564), where she jokes it must have in some way inspired her destiny: the hospital where she was born was later transformed into her town's City Hall. Maybe this is where her passion for community began, literally at birth.

Sylvia's mission in life is to challenge people all across the country to engage themselves in their communities, no matter what size. NewCities is a national non-profit organization that she launched in 2001 to help towns and cities all across the country to build social and economic vitality, regardless of their size and location. In addition to this position, Sylvia also serves as executive director of the Kentucky League of Cities (KLC).

I got to know her years ago when she gave a presentation to the Kentucky Association for Economic Development in Lexington, Kentucky. We had invited her as our featured speaker to talk about NewCities and trends across America.

Not having met Sylvia personally or heard her speak, I had no real expectations. Sylvia is a petite woman, which surprised me because when I had seen her interviewed on television or her photo in various magazines, she seemed tall. However, when this small-statured woman got up to the podium and started to speak I was shocked at the big voice and big words coming out of such a tiny person. I suddenly realized why people often refer to her as a "five-foot firecracker." She may be small, but she talks big and immediately challenged everyone in the room to become engaged in their communities. She was good. She was so good that I couldn't wait to get back to my office to spread the word and to start implementing some ideas that had temporarily been shelved. She had motivated me to encourage my organizations to get involved and become part of the process to tackle the challenges in this 21st century.

So now whenever Sylvia speaks, I listen because she is a walking encyclopedia of knowledge as it relates to towns of all sizes all across the country.

The KLC does not have a specific definition of a small town; however, Sylvia says that she has come to believe that a small town evokes perhaps more about the values and warmth than it does about size.

Sylvia says, "Cities and communities are organic in nature. Their DNA is about their individuality and their success. Small towns are coming back in style as we enter into a new age of localism." She says people are now rejecting the cold flickering computer screen in the middle of the night in favor of something new and different, and that is often the warm nurturing environment presented by many small towns. But will they move there? According to Sylvia, "It is said that most Americans will settle in just eight super regions by the year 2050. While I don't necessarily think that is true, given the down economy and the turn away from consumerism and the growth of new localism, small places do have a chance to thrive."

There was much debate that went in determining, for the sake of this book, what I was going to define as a small town. There really does not seem to be an official consensus of what defines a small town by population. You can research for hours (Google, Yahoo and the Nelson County Public Library are my new best friends) and discover that there is a wide array of definitions of what a small town is. Actually this is no different from what your friends or family may think a small town is also. I bet if you asked people from various size communities, all across the country, they would each give you a different opinion on what they consider a small town.

For instance, let's use some examples of some incredible places I have visited. If you asked someone in New York City, New York (Pop. Over 8 million), their idea of a small town may be Denver, Colorado (Pop. 588,000). And if you asked someone from Denver what their idea of a small town is, they may say Richmond, Virginia (Pop. 202,000). If you asked someone from Richmond, they may say Jackson, Wyoming (Pop. 9,631). Well, I could go on and on with this, but I think you can see where I am going. So, outside the academic definition, your personal definition may be something totally different and relative to where you live and the size of your town or city. So with that said, do you think you live in a small town?

After surveying mayors, county judges, those who deal with census figures regularly and everyday ordinary people from big and small towns alike, I came up with what an appropriate definition of a small town for my book. There seemed to be a consensus that when a town reaches populations of fifteen to twenty thousand it doesn't seem so small anymore, although I am sure there are exceptions to the rule. So for this book, the definition of a small town will be around fifteen thousand people or less.

While many small towns have gone unchanged in the last century, many flourishing farming communities have lost population and their emphasis on agriculture. In the early 1900s, it seemed most everyone lived in a small town and most of the economic base was centered on farming. There were even towns that had more cattle than residents. Today, less than five percent of the population is farmers and many of those farmers are finding it necessary to supplement those jobs with other income. Most of our livestock farms have been sold and have been developed as prime real estate. Where cattle once grazed, subdivisions have been built. Trees and forests are being cleared for industrial parks, commercial purposes, and for new highways that often reroute traffic away from the heart of the community.

Of course, we all know at least one of those "used-to-be" small towns that, because of factors like interstates and bypasses, are no longer recognizable as small towns because their town limits end on the fringe of the adjacent big city. It's a nasty little thing called "sprawl" that has changed the rural integrity of so many communities across the country.

Today, many of the successful small towns have cultivated their own niche when it comes to their economic wants and needs.

There are towns that survive because they are bedroom communities for larger cities, towns that focus on manufacturing as their economic base, towns with highly affluent colleges and even towns that are successful because of a military base nearby. And then, God love 'em, there are those tiny towns that are no more than what I call a "reduce-your-speed, drive-by-place-on-your-way-to-somewhere-else" small town. A town with sometimes no more than an aluminum 3 ft. x 2 ft. road sign with a name on it. I knew a town just like that in an adjoining county from where I grew up. As a game, my older brother and I would always have a contest to hold our breath from one end of town to the other. It really wasn't hard to do—the town was so small that most of the time we had enough breath still in us to get us about a mile out of town. The only times we were unsuccessful would be when we would look at each other right after we took that huge breath with our cheeks full of air. We resembled chipmunks that had just filled their mouths with nuts in preparation for the winter season. Because we looked so ridiculous, we would bust out laughing and would barely make it past the aluminum sign.

I have to admit that one of my favorite small towns doesn't fit into any of these categories. Telluride, Colorado (Pop. 2,360) is a quaint little mountain town in the southwestern corner of Colorado, known for its skiing, film and music festivals. It is also the part-time home to many celebrities. Nestled in a box canyon in the San Juan Mountains, Telluride is small in population, but don't let that fool you. It has a cosmopolitan feel with its upscale shops and sophisticated restaurants, and has a very healthy year-round allure for visitors. One of my favorite things about Telluride is that despite the upscale nature of the community, the residents and shop owners are very inviting and you get an immediate sense of community the minute you drive in town. You feel like a relative who has been invited back for a homecoming.

So what kind of small town do you live in? Just think about it for a second. If a stranger sitting next to you on a plane asked you to describe the town you are from, what would you say? What terms would you use and what characteristics would you highlight? Would you tell them a funny story about this town or describe its crazy characters? Maybe you'd tell them about your downtown and its great old buildings. This is always a good exercise to make you think about what gives your town its personality.

*H*ow do you become an expert on the allure of small towns? Just ask Jack Schultz and he will tell you. Schultz is the author of *Boomtown USA*, probably the most popular book today that promotes some of the best small towns in the U.S. and challenges communities to promote innovative thinking to revitalize themselves in this ever-changing economy.

Schultz says, "I believe the main allure to small towns today is they all have their own sense of place, and that is appealing. The ability to get out of the rat race of the big city and to slow down in the natural beauty of a smaller community is attracting more people back to the country." He is quick to point out that it doesn't happen that easily and that communities have to put plans in place and have the amenities to sustain a lifestyle that many people have become accustomed to in larger areas.

To maintain this small town appeal, Schultz goes on to point out that smart communities are beginning to understand that there is a paradigm shift happening in economic development: "We must spend less time looking for that big elephant company and more time on retaining the jobs we have in our towns today," he says. "But most importantly, small towns are going to need to work to grow our new entrepreneurs, people who want to work for themselves and have deeper roots within the community."

When asked who is doing it right, Schultz says there are many towns that are good examples, including a few of his favorites like Pagosa Springs, Colorado; Mooresville, North Carolina; Paducah, Kentucky; Leavenworth, Washington; Cape Girardeau, Missouri; and Columbus, Mississippi.

"If small towns don't take action to keep up with the bigger and more successful communities, they will slowly just age in place," he says. "When you have more deaths in your town than you do births then you know you are in trouble."

Schultz had these few suggestions for small town leaders:

1. Bring youth back to your community and put plans in place to attract the next generation.
2. Fix up your downtown and bring back that hustle and bustle of a community.
3. Make your town amenity-rich with broadband, video conferencing and good cell tower service.
4. Make your town unique. People, young and old are looking to live in a place unlike another.

Schultz is right on every point. Small towns need to take notice if they want to compete and to survive.

*I*t's important for me to say that this book is not only intended to entertain those who live in a small town, but anyone from East Coast to West Coast (and anywhere in between.) If you don't and never have lived in a small town, I will bet that at some time, somewhere, you have had a small town experience that is still stored in your memory just aching to be awakened.

Whatever your connection is to a small town, I hope this book will arouse some good memories and maybe even entice you to get off the couch or turn off your computer, hop in your vehicle and take off to the discover life on the extraordinary byways of America.

As you read this book, please know that it is not intended as a travel guide or even a relocation primer, though I hope you will enjoy getting to know the people and their towns that are featured. *Small Town Sexy* is simply intended to enlighten you about the wonderful lives that many of us are enjoying in small town America, and hopefully to change any of those dreaded perceptions that you may have to the contrary. My ultimate goal is to convince you that, just maybe, small town America is truly a sexy place to live.

SMALL TOWN *Sexy is realizing that a town's population figures are just numbers that have no bearing on the kind of life you can live there.*

Wow—now that sounds impressive!

However, to put it in the words of my daughter Meg when she was in middle school, "My mom makes Bardstown a better place to live and work." Simple and to the point.

I have defined my job this way ever since.

I subscribe to a quote I heard once while conducting a job interview, "Do a job you love and you will never have to work a day in your life." And if you're lucky to be doing that job, in a town you love, that's like the cherry on top.

Every day that I go to work, I feel that I have the greatest job in the world. Wait, I need to revise that statement: I have the greatest job in North America, but the second greatest job in the world. The best job in the world would be the one that advertised on Australia's tourism department website last year.—the job was for a caretaker of a small tropical island in Australia near the Great Barrier Reef. Now get this: your job description included overseeing the island by walking the beaches, keeping a watch on the reef and conversing with the world via blogs and videos about your experiences. Oh yeah, and you had to be able to speak English.

I was the perfect candidate!

I had worked in tourism and economic development, I speak English, and as my friends will attest to, I certainly know my way around a beach. I can also blog, Facebook, Skype and Twitter with the best of them. To my benefit, I'm a Pisces (a lover of water) so surrounding myself with the Coral Sea was my destiny. I'm in!

Well, I applied, but never heard a word. They ended up hiring a British guy for the position. I guess my lack of snorkeling experience could have taken me out of the running for the job. I am a bit claustrophobic, and can't imagine having a mask and plastic tube to rely on to help me breathe. Underwater sports may have been a prerequisite for that whole Barrier Reef thing. Oh well, I wish that British guy the best of luck.

Anyway, in the second best job in the world, as an economic developer in Bardstown and Nelson County, Kentucky, part of my job is having the pleasure to convince people that Bardstown and the other great small towns in the county are the absolute best places in the world for them to either live, locate a company or grow their business. If you know anything at all about my town, it is not a real hard sell. I know my counterparts in larger cities across the country have bigger salaries and more elaborate benefits, but there are some perks that go along with this job that are more attractive to me than country club memberships or expense accounts. My fringe benefits include wide-open spaces, clean air to breathe, a short commute (there is only one stoplight between my house and my office), a not-so-hectic way of life and working with people whose families, for generations, have called this wonderful little town "home."

Simply put, it is one of the most wonderful places in the U.S., which is evident by all the accolades we have received over the years included being listed in the publications *The 100 Best Small Towns in America* and *50 Best Small Southern Towns*. We have also been listed in *Where to Retire Magazine* and *National Geographic's Adventure and Traveler* publications.

Travel writers love small towns and the feeling is mutual. We love it when a travel writer calls and says they want to visit Bardstown because they have heard so much about us. Travel writer visits are like hosting a favorite relative you haven't seen in years and you want everything to be just right, with everyone on their best behavior and with picture perfect weather.

Bardstown is home to My Old Kentucky Home State Park, made famous by the Stephen Foster song of the same name. The song says "Oh, the sun shines bright on My Old Kentucky Home."—because we think, despite what's lingering in the skies, it shines in our spirit here every day of the year.

We can always tell when a travel writer's story about Bardstown has been published because our phone rings off the hook and our website's visits start to spike. Travel writers have a great job. I would call it the third best job in the world, just behind that Australian island caretaker I told you about earlier and my job, of course. What fun it would be traveling across the country writing about some of the coolest places around, and being treated like someone's favorite long-lost relative once you are there. Then, in addition to that, getting paid for it.

BS reporter and correspondent Charles Kuralt was one of my favorite broadcasters of all time. In his *On the Road* television series he traveled across the back roads of America in an RV to showcase the beauty of the countryside and its people in a way that most networks had not considered. These vignettes spotlighted what I consider to be true Americana, based on lives of good common people.

This program was the inspiration for a television series I developed and hosted in the 1990s called *On Location*. It was my own little *On the Road* series. I didn't get to cross the country, but I did sometimes cross my county lines. I didn't get an RV, but I did have an SUV. I also had a master cameraman and editor, John Coulter, who made filming the reality of life into an art. Getting to know the characters and places that not everyone knew about was a joy. Still today, people will approach me and comment about that program. They sometimes have specific questions like, "I loved that segment you did on that old covered bridge in Washington County. I have always wanted to visit it; can you tell me how to get there?" Or "I never knew there was a cave under our town. I have taken my son there twice since seeing your program." The program focused on our people and our places and we never ran out of stories to tell.

I miss hosting that program because it enabled me to see the "off-the-beaten-path" locations and meet people that I would not have otherwise been able to and allowed me to make many new friends along the way.

This leads into my dream job of the future. When I retire or win the lottery, whichever comes first, I want to become a travel writer/videographer and visit every small town I have ever read or heard about, and produce a travel series titled something like, *America's Most Livable and Lovable Small Towns*. Or how about a show named *America's Sexiest Small Towns*? I think I like the way that sounds.

I'm a Travel Channel junkie and love to watch those shows featuring the most exotic places in the world to visit, so why not feature places that are more obtainable and affordable, like sexy small towns in the U.S.?

What do you think?

*I*t's an April morning and the sun has come out from what has seemed to be an eternity's worth of overcast skies and rain. The temperature is rising into a comfortable fifty degrees, the dogwood trees are opening their white and pink blossoms, the grass is turning a vibrant green, and people are once again coming out of their winter hibernation. I can see it all because, as I tell anyone who comes to my rather large corner office, I have a wonderful "window to the world."

I work in the county's most iconic and picturesque structure, the Old Courthouse Building, circa 1892. It is literally located in the center of town. When I say literally, I mean it sits, like so many courthouses of its day, flat dab in middle of the road with a highway roundabout circling the building. The four corners of property on each side are known as our town's Court Square. Like so many small towns of years ago, it's the area where the courthouse offices and small town attorneys conducted their daily legal business. In 2004, a new Justice Center was built east of the downtown area and all the court offices were moved from the center of town. Fortunately, for the sake of the community's vitality, most of the attorneys remained downtown. It was then that my economic development offices of Chamber of Commerce, Main Street organization, office of Tourism and Industrial and Economic Development relocated to the Old Courthouse, giving a new and appropriate use for this grand old structure that we now know as the county's official "Welcome Center."

My office in the Old Courthouse is the former home of county judge executives and district court judges, those who deserved grandeur in their surroundings. At one time the windows were bullet proof—protection for the judges against anyone who might hold a grudge about not-so-popular sentences that may have been handed down over the years.

As I sit there at night, when it is quiet and traffic outside has calmed, I can sometimes sense the history made in this building. I can almost hear the characters that have come and gone throughout the decades; I sometime wish these walls could talk. Oh, what small town stories they could tell.

I look out my four massive eight-foot-high windows and can see north all the way down our main street probably four to five blocks, and west as far as our historic Basilica of St. Joseph Proto-Cathedral. Each morning after I arrive at my office and open this wonderful old building for another day, I see Haydon Spalding, the local clothing store owner sweeping his sidewalk, preparing to open his shop as generations of Spaldings have done for more than 150 years. I watch and often admire the local stay-at-home moms, who have dropped their children off at school, out for their daily power walk with "the girls." I watch as guests pack their cars after an overnight stay at the Old Jailers Inn and wonder if they enjoyed their "captivating" experience in this real jail turned bed and breakfast. Probably one of my favorite sights each morning is watching the "good ol' boys" of Nelson County, who come and go in shifts to our local downtown diner, to share stories of events that have occurred within the last twenty-four hours and to jokingly harass any willing politician who dares to enter that particular morning.

And that roundabout—that crazy no-nonsense roadway that circles my building like a psychotic merry-go-round leading to all points east, west, north and south. These old courthouses and court squares were at one time popular designs in small towns, though today's transportation officials often scratch their heads and wonder what their counterparts of yesteryear were thinking. While they are designed to move traffic freely around the Court Square, this particular one has flaws. I know all too well about these flaws, because while sitting at my desk, I am only a thirty-foot strip of lawn away from the highway.

At least once an hour I will hear the screeching of tires as perfectly intelligent drivers attempt to master this roundabout. I always thought road rage was reserved for big city drivers, but let me tell you, we do have our share in small town America and sometimes we are not nice people. I will hear some aggressive horn honking outside my window only to look up just in time to see a driver, signaling to another, that he is "number one" with his middle finger. Or watching out-of-town-drivers, so intimidated by the whole roundabout thing that they get flustered not knowing which way to go, and maneuver the roundabout backwards.

My assistant Kim, (yes, we have the same name, and, yes, it does cause some confusion) will hear me yell, "No! No, don't do it." She will run into my office expecting to see someone pointing a gun to my head, only to realize I am standing in my window waving my hands and yelling at the car outside my office circling the roundabout the wrong way and heading dead straight for another car. I can fortunately say that we do not have many accidents, but several yield signs fall victim just about every month.

Despite all the horn honking, road rage, and sign mowing that goes with this roundabout, it is considered to be a sort of "character" in our town, an icon that is part of everyone's history. It holds lots of memories for many people, including me and anyone else who grew up driving in Nelson County in the 60s and 70s. During many years, it was part of the student driver's test course, and why not? To go anywhere in town, you have to go around it and if you could maneuver it without incident, you deserved a driver's license for life.

The roundabout also became a late night ritual to many high school students. Almost like an initiation, you weren't part of the "in crowd" until you had the nerve to go around the Courthouse backwards, and without getting caught by the police. This was such a cultural experience that when Bardstown celebrated its 225th birthday in 2005, then Mayor Dixie Hibbs came up with a fund raising idea to actually close a lane of traffic late one evening and allow people to drive around the Courthouse backwards, this time legally. We did it and had a lot of fun; however, the adrenaline rush of getting caught was lacking since the police were there watching us, not chasing after us.

You have to love the simple things we do in small towns to amuse ourselves.

*O*kay, it's time for some "me" time. Time to talk a little bit about "me," so you get to know me, review my small townologist résumé, get into my head to try to figure out this crazy small town addiction, and to decide for yourself if an intervention is necessary.

I was born and raised in the charming town of Bloomfield, Kentucky. (Pop. 886). My brother Tiger, my only sibling, is two years older—unless you ask him, and he will swear he's the youngest.

Tiger is his nickname, and he will tell you he has never confirmed how he got it. However, I tell the story my Mom told about our grandfather, an Air Force pilot, who flew planes called "The Tigers." (We know this for sure.) So when Tiger was born, as the story goes, my grandfather called him his "Little Tiger." I swear that is how the story went, though Tiger disputes it.

His real name is Davis Lee Huston, III, named for my grandfather and father. As vice president of one of the largest banks in the area, he works with the most powerful and affluent in the region. After five, he goes home to the town we both grew up in and to the stately home our triple-great-grandfather, Spence Minor, built in 1813. Behind the suit and tie is one of the best music minds around. Tiger owns one of the largest and most impressive collections of rock and roll record albums I have ever seen. I told him, early on, that if the banking profession didn't work out, he could put his college journalism degree to work and have a great career with Rolling Stone magazine. He is everyone's "go to guy" for any good music mix or any rock and roll question of the past three decades. He came by this love of music early as the manager for a group of his best friends who started a band in the basement of the church next door to where we were raised. "Tequila Sunrise" was our small town equivalent of Creedence Clearwater Revival. The band would play for all of our special events, including our dances and nights at the skating rinks. For years, I was their best groupie and had crushes on every member of the band.

We have laughed over the years because Tiger always compared our small town upbringing to that of the popular television series *Ozzie and*

Harriett. I would say it is *Ozzie and Harriett* meets *Leave it to Beaver* with a little bit of the cartoon series *The Jetsons* thrown in. The latter is due to the fact that my Dad was a gadget-guy like George Jetson.

We lived a very normal American lifestyle in a simple house on Main Street just up from the post office. We shared our home with a grandmother I adored, an aquarium full of fish and a series of misfit dogs, including a toy poodle, Old English sheepdog and a bird dog named "Bird Dog." I would get the oddest looks yelling his name when he went lost.

My family also consisted of Geneva, who was our housekeeper, my grandmother's caretaker and our babysitter. She was a second mother to me, as she was there five days a week and taught me how to iron, clean house and cook. Geneva was also the unfortunate one to have to deal with my brother and me when our parents were gone, especially every Thursday night when my parents would join their friends in Bardstown for dinner at the country club.

My specialty was sneaking my grandmother's Ford LTD out of the driveway and taking it for a spin around the block when I was fourteen. I managed to get by with this for several months by turning the volume up on the television show my grandmother and Geneva were watching in hopes they could not hear me start the car. The day finally came when my parents returned one evening, sooner than expected, and my dad, walking past the car felt heat coming from the its hood. Knowing my grandmother was not able to drive anymore and Geneva had never driven a day in her life, it had to be me. Busted!

I was a tomboy growing up and later a sort-of-a-jock, a by-product of living with a dad who played and coached several high school sports and with a very athletic mother. My mom never met a sport she didn't like. She is a great golfer, and a tiger on the tennis court and a master of the jack knife off a diving board.

She also learned how to swim like a fish in Herrington Lake near Danville, Kentucky. I remember she had the most beautiful swim stroke and would just glide across the water so effortlessly. It was these inherent good genes that gave me the ability to play many sports, including basketball, softball, track, golf, tennis, cheerleading and gymnastics.

However, I was one of those who could play every sport and master none. I was not bad at golf in high school, and for a while really enjoyed it.

However, my social life got in the way, and I preferred my weekends with my boyfriend instead of being trapped on a golf course in a tournament with strangers much older than me. I whined ever minute I was on the course, thought about all my friends at field parties in the country, cruising the main drag and that I was missing it all. I know my dad was disappointed when I gave up golf as he has hoped someday to retire as my caddy on the Women's PGA Tour.

My dad ended up playing a significant role in my cheerleading years during high school. On three occasions, he was summoned to the gymnasium to scrape me up off the floor and take me to the hospital when I had fallen from the top of a three-person stunt. I was knocked out cold twice and suffered four concussions. Let's not mention the broken bones and shin splints that came with my six years of cheerleading. My dad's athletic training came in handy. Before each game, he would tape me up like an NFL running back, so I could cheer another game.

I lived the stereotypical small town life in Bloomfield—church on Sunday, yard sale each spring, going to summer recreation programs, to chili suppers and fish fries, and hosting numerous lemonade stands. I was an event planner at age twelve and would host fairs and game night in my backyard like the PTA socials we had in school. While waiting for my Mom to get off from her job at school, I would dig through the garbage cans behind the school and salvage things that teachers had thrown away. To supplement my small allowance, I would go door-to-door in my neighborhood and sell those big green, what I called "hedge apples," for a nickel, guaranteed to ward off any spiders if you put them in your closets. With the money I earned, I would buy more games, which allowed me an even bigger fair and better prizes. My friends would come because they each knew they would leave with a free prize. My entrepreneurial spirit was apparent from an early age; I loved it!

During my years growing up, in the 1960s and 1970s, Bloomfield was a small agricultural town, known at that time for our tobacco warehouses and the festival we would hold every October to celebrate this commodity. The highlights of the Tobacco Festival were the parade and Tobacco Festival Queen contest—but what brought onlookers from all over the state was the tobacco-spitting contest. Yes, you read that right, a contest for the best tobacco-spitter in the state.

I can remember vividly a group of older men, mostly dressed in bib overalls. They would bring their families to cheer them on and the event would draw dozens of on-lookers. Second to the parade, this contest was the most popular event of the weekend.

Tobacco was a way of life in my world, as it was in so many rural towns across the South. Everyone smoked and it was not frowned upon because it was what our local economy was based on and what paid our bills. My parents smoked, my grandmother smoked, and my grandfather chewed tobacco. In my hometown, we lived those days when tobacco was king and for miles, all you could see was row after row of tobacco fields.

Tobacco season was an exciting time in farming communities like Bloomfield—our tobacco warehouses were busy with farmers bringing their crop to be sold and buyers from all across the country would be there to assess and bid on the crop. Bloomfield's population seemed to double during these weeks.

In my eyes, Bloomfield was a postcard-perfect small town. It had enough retail and commerce to take care of all your basic needs without having to leave town. Gas stations, grocery stores, clothing stores, a jewelry shop, laundromat, hardware store, diners, a florist, a dry cleaner, a drug store, and other small stores lined our downtown. I was too young to remember, but my parents often told me that the Bloom Theatre was the most popular place in town to go—to see a movie or host a special event. I do, however, remember the Gypsy Drive-In that was only fifteen minutes away. Two things stand out in my memory about the drive-in: they had the greatest giant dill pickles in the county and somehow, I lost a brand new pair of cheerleading shoes there.

Bloomfield was also the home to the Sutherland Mill, which was one of the largest employers at one time. A flour and corn mill operation, the company was run by generations of the Sutherland family in Bloomfield. Their most popular product, Kentucky Colonel Seasoned Flour, is still famous on a national level and has been compared to the Colonel's popular Kentucky Fried Chicken secret recipe with all sorts of wonderful herbs and spices.

This magical seasoned flour can make even the worst cook look good. Not that I would know, of course. But, I have been known to whip up some mean sausage gravy with this flour that would make even the best of Southern cooks envious. This was our "claim to fame" business in town. We loved the fact that Bloomfield's name was on every one of their product labels in every store around.

Both of my parents were educators. My dad was a teacher, high school coach and school administrator and my mom was an elementary school secretary. She always told me there wasn't a child's knee in Bloomfield she hadn't bandaged.

For the majority of their careers, both worked at the local schools just blocks from our house. Working in the field of education did have its perks. My parents enjoyed their summers off along with my brother and me. These three months of vacation allowed us the summer to do things as a family that included driving from one end of the state to the other visiting Kentucky's great state park system. We also spent a considerable amount of time in Florida visiting my aunt and uncle and weeks at Herrington Lake in Danville.

When you grow up in a small town, you don't have the opportunities to participate in some of the "finer things" that are only available in the bigger communities. We didn't have much access to the arts, to movies and certainly not to museums. The talents that we had were inherent, self–taught, or as a result of being taught by very talented local people.

As with most parents, my mother always had high hopes for me. She was sure that I would inherit her family's musical talents and be able to sing, dance and play every instrument. To help move me along in her quest for my stardom, she signed me up for every lesson that was being taught in Bloomfield, including tap, ballet, and piano lessons.

After six months of tap lessons, I came in second place in a 4-H dance competition with a tap dance to the song "Mame" and can still remember my instructor Mr. Bob (who by the way looked just like the television show Batman's Adam West) mouthing the words to my dance routine steps off stage, "shuffle, ball change, heel step, shuffle, ball change, heel step, buffalo, buffalo."

The only way to describe my performance would be to compare it with the clumsy scarecrow in *The Wizard of Oz*, attempting to skip his way down the yellow brick road. The first place winner was Margaret Sue Cornell with her black tuxedo-like costume and top hat. I think she won every contest after that.

Okay, so I wasn't going to make a living on Broadway with my tap dancing. Next came ballet.

I was a tomboy and a bit of a jock since the day I could walk, so I wasn't the most graceful person in tights and a tutu. Somehow, my mom had convinced Mr. Bob to be my ballet instructor. Even as a child, I could sense his reluctance in wanting to instruct me. He would give a lot of attention to the tall and slender girls who seem to float across the floor. I, on the other hand, did not float, and actually thought the whole ballet thing was a bit prissy.

Despite my bad attitude about ballet, I did place third in my one and only ballet recital and I got a ribbon for my performance. Of course, there were only three competing in my age group.

There would be no Sugar Plum Fairy role for me that year.

Next on the list were piano lessons—something my Mom knew I would excel at due to the fact that most of her relatives played the piano beautifully. My parents invested $500 in a piano and over $100 in piano lessons, to the dismay of my father who had to pay for them and my brother who had to listen to me practice the scales for an hour each day. After six months of lessons and two recitals (my recitals pieces were "Battle Hymn of the Republic" and "Greensleeves"), the unthinkable occurred. I was respectfully fired by my piano teacher, Alice Snider, who by the way, was my best friend Barbara's mother, and like a second mother to me.

I loved going to Barbara's house. It was like hanging out with the popular television family *The Partridge Family*, but on a smaller scale. They were all so talented and could sing and play the piano so beautifully. I wanted to be a Partridge.

My teacher Alice, and her mother Nana, were the best piano teachers in town and were always asked to play piano or organ for any event that was held, including church events, weddings and funerals. They loved me like their own, but knew if they couldn't teach me, it just was not meant to be.

I saw my dad break a smile the day we sold the piano.

It was at that moment that my mom came to the ultimate conclusion that the Gabbard musical gene must have skipped a generation.

For nine years, I went to school in Bloomfield with the same kids I started first grade with, including some of my best friends Barbara, Randy, Johnnie, Kathy, Sherry, Terry and Gary. My school career began at Eli Brown Elementary School for four years, then Bloomfield Junior High School for fifth through ninth grade.

In small towns, families are nearby with grandparents, aunts and uncles and dozens of cousins right up the street or just outside of town. Families stay close, because we live so close. Even if we are not related, we act like an extended family because we are connected in so many ways. We walk to school together, cheer and play ball together, and spend our weekends together at the events of our school or community. I loved my weekends at the skating rink, which was the social arena for the kids in our area. We owned our own skates and made colorful fuzzy balls that would attach onto the laces. Most of our first girl- and boy-friend relationships came from our nights at the rink.

Our junior high school ended at ninth grade and for our sophomore through senior years, we would be forced to leave the comfort of who and what we knew, and our close-knit small town school, to travel ten miles to attend Nelson County Senior High School, in Bardstown. School consolidation occurred all across Kentucky in the late 1960s and early 70s.

We were about to the leave our comfort zone.

The girls I cheered against and the boys on the opposing teams, the ones that I had grown to know as rivals, would now be sitting next to me in class. We would now be on the same team.

After about five months of getting to know each other and erasing our turf lines, school had gone from tolerable to enjoyable. I had acquired new friends from small towns in the county that I did not even know existed before, like New Hope, Boston, Deatsville, Balltown and Howardstown. These were towns even smaller than mine.

I went on to the University of Kentucky (Go Big Blue!) for my college education in the mid-sized town of Lexington, Kentucky, and we will learn more about how I fared there a little later.

Those years were great, but the small town girl in me wouldn't go away, even after discovering a new exciting life in a bigger city.

I returned back to small town America and started a radio broadcasting career in Bardstown, Kentucky (Pop. 11,000), which is about fifteen minutes from my hometown. From Bardstown, I never left, and tried not to look back on that distant glow of the big city lights in College Town, U.S.A.

This small pond is where this small fish is destined to swim and, hopefully, grow bigger in size in the years to come.

I've never been sure if there was that one experience buried deep in my subconscious that led me to feel so strongly about wanting a life in a small town. There may be a few out there who would love to psychoanalyze this obsession, but honestly it doesn't matter. I love where I have been and where I am, and I wouldn't want to be anywhere else (except, maybe, on the beach of that small island in Australia).

SMALL TOWN *Sexy is having a passion about the place you live and knowing if you go away, you can always come home.*

can only happen hundreds or thousands of miles away from home, and in exotic places that usually cost a lot to get to. I am here to tell you that some of my most memorable trips have taken place in towns even smaller than my own.

I became a small town junkie in the 1990s when I began traveling out west to hike and backpack in the states of Colorado, Arizona, Utah, New Mexico, Wyoming and Montana. I made a vow to myself that I would not, except for emergency purposes, find my way on to an interstate highway—my destination would be by way of the state roadways of our past for hundreds of miles. Two-lane roads that have stories to tell and I want to hear them all.

There is an excitement for me as I travel, finding my way off the busier highways of America and back to the scenic byways, traveling like my parents did before there were major interstates and those dreaded by-passes that route you away from the soul of a town. A great website, sponsored by the National Scenic Byways Program, [part of the U.S. Department of Transportation and Federal Highway System (www. byways.org)] specifically maps out some of the most travel-worthy roadways in the U.S. Whenever I know I am going to be in a certain part of the country, I will jump on this website and find the most scenic or culturally-interesting route to my destination.

I love discovering a new small town, finding my way to its Main Street, its central business district or whatever seems to be the heart of that community. They are not hard to find because they are usually filled with flags flying on light poles or cute little banners spotlighting an upcoming event. I love to wander the streets, lunch at local restaurants, browse the stores and if they have an active industrial base, I will visit their business parks. (I'm sure that sounds boring, but that's the economic developer in me.)

Ordinarily, I would not share this, because it sounds a bit odd, but I even like visiting their cemeteries—but mind you, not in a haunting or morbid way. You can learn a lot about a town and its history from reading the epitaphs in a cemetery. There are great stories to be told about the long-past famous as well as the infamous residents of these towns.

But most of all (and probably my favorite) you can find out a lot about a town and its character by having a drink where the locals hang out and getting to know the people, and in all probability, the "characters" in that community. Although some of these establishments may look quaint inside with their dart boards, juke boxes and pinball machines, you really have to use caution, good judgment, and more importantly common sense, on selecting the appropriate dives to wander into. And let me give you this one little word of warning on being too social when in an unfamiliar town: not everyone enjoys having strangers snuggle up to them at their favorite bar to have a drink and especially, not to have conversation. My hope to acquire some local wisdom and genius from these folks has not always turned out well, and I will just leave it at that.

Much like our own individual human characteristics, every community has its own character that it has taken years to define. These traits and personalities are as different as the towns themselves.

There are just some details that we must all agree on before we continue. Many small towns can be quite charming; while others, well, not so much. That statement was not meant to offend any of small town enthusiasts out there, but to give an unbiased realization "that all small towns are not created equal."

Like I said earlier, *Small Town Sexy* is an allure, an appeal, and a seductive charm that makes you keep coming back. Towns exist for all sorts of reasons, and we all have our own ideas of what makes a town worth coming back to. Sometimes a town's charm centers on factors such as its recreational opportunities, like being near beaches, lakes or rivers. Maybe it's full of cultural offerings like museums, theatre and art galleries. Some towns are known for their historical nature, like being the home of a famous person, the location of a famous event, or being filled with beautiful historic buildings dating back centuries. And of course, many small towns are known and loved for their natural scenic beauty including forests and mountains.

And let's be honest, there are those small towns that don't really fit into one particular category and have no specific character, but nonetheless, are special in their own way to those people who live there and call these towns "home." I call these towns "NTBs." They are Nice Towns, But . . . I am not sure I want to live here. This was coined after a sorority phrase we used for guys we were not interested in dating in college. They were called "NGBs." Nice Guys, But . . . we don't want to go out with them. They were great guys, who were a lot of fun, and whom we wanted as our friends, but not as boyfriends. I think you get my assessment. Many residents in these types of towns have a true sense of community pride and confidence and honestly couldn't care less about what people thought about their hometown.

*I*f you rank towns on a success level, those with economy and population on the rise, they have one thing in common. They have a vision of what they want their town to become and have set their sights in that direction. Some towns aspire to become a tourism destination, so they invest in new attractions; some hope to grow their industrial base, so they spend time recruiting; and others are putting plans in place for the next great "green community" and are investing in a new, efficient state-of-the-art infrastructure. We usually read about those towns with a distinctive vision and with leaders who vow to make it—those towns are success stories.

I have heard it said many times that where we grow up defines who we are. It's the influence of the culture and our environment that helped mold who we are today. While I have not been able to find much research to substantiate this statement, I can base that comment personally on experience and from the opinions of others whose passions for small towns are just as strong as mine.

A common theme I have found in my studies of those who live in smaller and more rural communities is that they have a work ethic like no other. Growing up on a farm, you worked 24/7, were up at daylight and your day didn't end until the sun went down. There were no sick days, and very little vacation. It is this kind of work ethic that most will never experience in our lives.

My Nelson County Judge Executive Dean Watts enjoys explaining our "good ol' boy" logic to people who visit our county for the first time. "We have good, hard-working people in Nelson County," says Judge Watts. "Many were born and raised on a farm where people had to teach themselves how to get things done. When a tractor breaks down in the field, you can't wait for AAA to send a truck. We are forced to learn how to do these things ourselves. Because of this, we have an entire society of folks who understand this work ethic and the fundamentals of getting things done."

This early initiation into a life of hard work has merited much success with companies that have been fortunate to hire these hard-working, small town individuals.

❧❧

We have our share of home-grown success stories and are proud of those who have gone on to achieve some degree of greatness. We wear our pride on our sleeves and when we have something or someone to show off, we do it big for all to see.

Take, for instance, our city limit signs. We all have them as a sort of bragging billboard to tell you not only the name of the town you just crossed into, but a little bit about what makes us unique. "Welcome to Small Town U.S.A, Home of the 1978 Girls State Champion Softball Team," or "Welcome to Small Town U.S.A, Home of Janie Doe, 1983 Third Runner-Up in the Miss USA Pageant." One I saw recently was in Lenoir City, Tennessee (Pop. 2,847) read, "1958 State Champions." 1958? This pride has lived for decades! This is small town self-promotion at its best.

And God bless the towns that have real life, homegrown celebrities and heroes like Perryville, Kentucky (Pop. 763), which proudly boasts as you enter their town that they are the "Home of Eddie Montgomery of the county music duo, Montgomery Gentry and is the town of their hit song, *This is My Town.*"

It seems most every small town has what they consider their own local hometown and home-grown famous celebrities or VIPs. Bardstown is no different. First and foremost, we are so proud that Stephen Foster visited his Bardstown relatives in the 1850s and was inspired to write the song *My Old Kentucky Home* based on his cousin's Federal Hill mansion and plantation. The song was eventually adopted as Kentucky's state song and the plantation was later designated as a Kentucky State Park. For over fifty years, we have been celebrating this great composer's music every summer during the outdoor performance of, *Stephen Foster—The Musical.*

In 2002, Mel Gibson starred in the American war film *We Were Soldiers.* That movie was based on a book about Lt. Gen. Hal Moore, who is from Bardstown and who led the first battle of military forces into the Vietnam War.

Although Lieutenant General Moore moved away from Bardstown years ago, he has family ties in Bardstown and still makes visits to our community. To show the respect and the pride that we have in our own American hero, our local leaders renamed a section of highway into town, Lt. Gen. Hal Moore Parkway. There are stories like this all over our country where towns pay homage to their own.

Like most kids in towns, big and small, we grow up having aspirations of becoming "someone" some day. Maybe we want to be a famous ball player or become a famous actress. Maybe we just want to be rich, not really caring how we get there. Unfortunately, a small percentage of us never achieve our dream. But, some do, and we just have to learn to live our life of fame through them, following their careers, and wishing them the greatest of success and at times, wishing we had their life. In my hometown, James Dean Hicks is one of those who had a dream and has followed it to success. He is one of our hometown boys "done good."

James Dean Hicks was born and raised on a 500-acre farm in Nelson County, Kentucky, between Greenbrier and Holy Cross. He was born into a family of hard-working, church-going, down-home people. James' parents loved naming their kids after famous people: James was named after movie star James Dean; another brother was named for John Wayne; and a third after Ernest Tubb. James says he guesses he is lucky because he could have been named Doris Day.

From an early age, we all knew James (known to us in his formative years as "Jimmy Dean") was destined to be in the country music business. At ten years of age, while most of us were deciding where to go for ice cream or who would have a sleep over that night, James was making an over-two-hour commute to Nashville, Tennessee, to perform in the "Country Music Capital of the World." His family knew if he was going to make it in this business, Nashville was where Jimmy Dean had to be.

And make it, he did. Everyone fell in love with little Jimmy Dean Hicks. Among the many places that he performed was the WSM *Radio Midnight Jubilee*, a show that every budding country music artist wanted to be on. Those persistent trips to Nashville eventually paid off as he was asked to perform with various country music artists like Tammy Wynette, George Jones, Conway Twitty and Loretta Lynn, legends in the industry today.

And it didn't take long until Nashville knew who little Jimmy Dean Hicks was. After high school at age seventeen plus a music degree from Western Kentucky University, he headed straight to Nashville to pursue his lifelong dream in country music. If you are a fan of country music you are certainly no stranger to James' music. His discology includes songs like "It Takes a Little Rain" and "This Crazy Love" performed by the Oak Ridge Boys, and "Goodbye Time" by Conway Twitty.

There's not a female country music fan out there who hasn't danced to one of James' most popular songs "Working Women Holiday," sung by Sammy Kershaw. That song became an instant anthem for working women all across America. It's those women who make up a large portion of James' fans, because of the heartwarming lyrics and the passion that is apparent in every song he writes. And yeah, every woman out there would be disappointed if I didn't mention his country good looks and long wavy hair, which has become his signature style.

But more importantly, and speaking from someone who has known him for years, James is just a good guy, who loves his family and still keeps in touch with his high school buddies.

If you listen to the lyrics in James' songs you can feel your life slow down and your favorite family memory becomes vivid in your mind. These are familiar themes to those of us who live in small town America.

James describes his memories like this: "Growing up in rural America and growing up on a farm determined the way I speak which is very 'country music' and very 'common man.' Some of my biggest songs were inspired by my years on the farm and in church. Songs like 'Jesus' and 'Momma Always Loved Me,' 'Heaven Help,' God Gave Me You' and 'A Bible and a Bus Ticket Home.' It's this Christian upbringing and my rural roots that filters in on so many of my songs."

Becoming one of the most sought-after songwriters and artists today, James has every reason to be a bit arrogant about his life and his career. He, by all means, is a true hotshot in the country music industry. But this is so far from who James is, what he stands for and how he was raised. He knows if he were to ever take on "hotshot" ways, he has family and friends back home who will straighten him out pretty quickly.

James was raised in a small modest house with seven other kids. "We never had very much, but we always had plenty to eat because we grew everything ourselves. I was not an 'entitlement' child, so it did not take a lot to make me happy. My parents instilled in us that you only deserve what you get out and work for, and this is what has guided my life," James recalls. "Nashville is a tough business and it is the one town that everyone goes to, to get their break in the business. While many do find their way, there are 100 times more that never do."

In Nashville it's not always about the talent, James says, but it's about the hard work and persistence and outworking people to make your way. James says he is used to working hard for what he got all his life, so his upbringing sort of laid a map for the rest of his life.

When you ask James what it is he misses about life in small town America, it doesn't take him but a second to answer that question, "The food! We had real live, organic food before it was ever in style, because that is how we grew our food on the farm. And I miss that terribly."

James will also admit to you that he misses the slower lifestyle, one that he hopes to return to one day, because it is the life that he really loves. "It's a funny thing about life—the first twenty years you find a way to get away from home and as you get a little older you spend the rest of it trying to find a way to get back."

He has a plan in mind—ever since James was a kid, he has had a dream to fix up an old log home on his farm (the same home where his grandparents grew up.) James is just hoping that his life will eventually slow down enough, so he will be able to fulfill this lifelong dream back at home on the farm in Nelson County.

"I wouldn't trade the way I grew up for anything. We grew up very rural. We did not have indoor plumbing, so I was the water boy and pumped water from the well every day. I was also the firewood boy because mom would cook on a woodstove."

"Back then I cursed that lifestyle because I felt everybody else had so much more and I really didn't have that much. It shaped who I was back then, which in some ways is good and in others, not so much."

James tells me that looking back, and being on the other side of things, that lifestyle made him appreciate what little he did have. "It takes very little to please me, I am very grateful for what I have and everything that comes to me in life. And I know that if everything I have worked so hard from were taken away tomorrow, I would survive. "

James says, "If there is anything I believe, I truly believe that being raised in a small town is the biggest thing that ever happened to me."

From the time he could sing his first song, James always knew what he wanted to do. He was one of the lucky ones who was able to complete his college career, pack his bags and head south to Nashville. He knew that to follow his dream that was where he had to be.

J understand following a dream and being where you need to be to make it happen. Sometimes, the dream takes you to a town or city where you don't want to be, but "need to be" for the sake of your job. Then there are those who know where they want to be and search out a profession only in that location. That is how it was for me—it just so happened that my dream after college brought me back home to my hometown in small town America.

After four years at the University of Kentucky and a wonderful and exciting part-time internship at WVLK Radio, one of the largest and most prestigious radio stations in Lexington, I returned home. I had amazing opportunities at WVLK as I assisted in producing UK sports programs, became involved in organizing concerts, was a production assistant and later promoted to weekend disc jockey (aka "Dusty Summers").

At that point in my life, I was living my college dream job—the envy of my classmates. I was learning from some of the best in the business including station manager and my mentor, Ralph Hacker, and my favorite sports guy, Dick Gabriel. Dick was right out of college himself and helped me through some of my "new intern" anxiety. Dick really turned me on to sports, and I would have loved to have had a career in sports broadcasting, but the opportunities at that time were very limited. An instinct for the "need to know" led me to an interest in news.

However, I still knew I was a small fish in a big ol' pond at that station and in that city. Though I had been there four years, it often seemed a bit overwhelming. So as graduation neared, I had a choice to make. Stay in big city radio, where I had been offered a full-time position, or go home and accept a job offer as news director at my hometown radio station—a place I had worked during my college summer breaks.

My love affair with my hometown led me back. Since that decision, I have realized how important the time I spent in the city was and that those amazing opportunities sent me in a direction I needed to go.

I turn around in my chair, and once again, I am mesmerized as I look out this big "window to the world" in my office. It allows me to see into the enormous heart of this small town. Being able to step out my door—and into this real-life streaming of small town life—has convinced me that there is a wonderful story to be told about the life, the experiences, the humor, and the drama that unfold every day in small town America.

As I pondered whether or not I thought I could write a book, a writer friend of mine said we all have a book in us just waiting to be written. I reminded him that while I was a broadcast journalist, writing a news story and writing a book are two very different things. To encourage this endeavor, he pulled out a little piece of paper and wrote something on it and gave it to me. He said, "Whenever you lose confidence in your ability to write, pull out this piece of paper and read it."

I looked down at the piece of paper and read what he had written, "You have to live it, to write it."

So simple, yet so true. God knows I live this wonderful small town life every day, so now's the time to share this feeling with the world

SMALL TOWN *Sexy* is the pride we have

in the place we live and in those who

have gone on to make us proud.

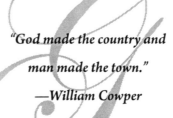

"God made the country and man made the town."
—William Cowper

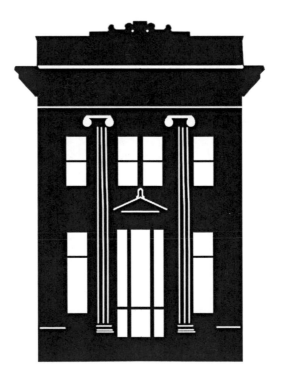

chapter four

IT'S NOT YOUR MAYBERRY ANYMORE

*W*here would we all be without the television shows of the 1960s and 70s, like the *Andy Griffith Show, Green Acres*, and *Petticoat Junction*, all set in sleepy, slow-paced little towns of Mayberry and Hooterville. These programs are iconic with their bigger-than-life characters like Sheriff Andy Taylor, Deputy Barney Fife, Uncle Joe of the Shady Rest Motel and Arnold Ziffle (the pig that understood English). We would turn on the television in an effort to escape from reality and be transported to a place where a former New York City attorney plowed his field in a suit and handymen came and went because no one locked their doors. I remember these shows could entertain us for hours. They took us back to a simple, less stressful kind of life.

The people who lived in Mayberry were more than characters to us. They were real people with real lives, living in a real place. For generations, we, too, lived with them in Mayberry.

If you never had the pleasure of growing up in a small town and experiencing small town realities, chances are your opinions and perceptions about life in a small town were formed by what you saw when your family gathered around the television for an evening of entertainment. To you, towns like Mayberry were stereotypical small towns that were home to one sheriff (with no gun), one gas station, and one local barbershop where all the men would hang out and gossip. A town full of characters, very little crime, and even fewer things to worry about.

Not unlike these shows of the past, small towns today still have their own cast of characters, though maybe not as colorful and flamboyant as Mayberry's own Otis the town drunk who knew how to check himself into jail after a night of indulgence, or Goober the auto mechanic who worked on every car in town at apparently the only gas station in town. How dull would these shows have been without these lovable characters?

The one thing that these television shows often did was give us a glimpse into a simpler life, probably less realistic, but very desirable. There were no reality shows and we didn't need them. We wanted something different to watch outside the lives that we were leading every day. These shows would pull us in so much that we often felt like part of their extended families.

And then one day it happened. I was watching a television show and realized that this was the life for me. It was no longer a television program, but a dream that I wanted to pursue.

I found my dream life on television in a beautiful small town in New England after becoming so enthralled with the 1980s sitcom *Newhart*, starring Bob Newhart. He played a New York City author who moved with his wife to Vermont to operate The Stratford Inn. This was what I would eventually do with my life—I was going to operate a cozy country inn in New England.

Newhart's character was very laid back and mild mannered. He was surrounded by a community of quirky misfits, including my favorite trio of brothers: Larry, Darryl and his other brother, Darryl. (I was always a bit curious about their parents and if they even had a last name.)

My favorite scenes were always when the town was suffering a crisis; the entire town would gather in city hall and meet with the mayor to determine its fate. That slapstick bickering among the townspeople could have been taken from a documentary of many small town meetings all across the U.S. I loved that town and that way of life, despite its eccentric residents.

There seemed to be a similar theme throughout each of these small town-inspired shows. The characters were very genuine. Usually it was "what you see is what you get." No pretense, no façade—these people seemed real and to the audience, they were. Because they were such beloved characters, we could sometimes sit and associate these characters to residents in our own towns. We all have our sometimes inept Barneys, and it is certain that every town has a sweet little relative like Aunt Bee. And can I have a show of hands of everyone who knew someone who looked just like Mayberry's little red-headed, freckle-faced Opie Taylor?

After talking with dozens of people while writing this book, I discovered that there are still many Mayberrys and Hootervilles that exist in America today. I say that quite affectionately. These small towns are home to residents who are as genuine as those characters we saw years ago on television. These small town residents count their blessings every day because they live where everyone moves just a bit slower, people talk just a little bit simpler, and where the streets roll up at dark.

*W*hile I was growing up, and throughout my college years, I never seemed to stay away from my own "Mayberry" for long.

When I was young, one of my favorite things to do was spend the weekend, without my parents, at my grandparents' home in Danville, an hour away. I was the only granddaughter, so I couldn't think of anything better than staying the weekend (alone) to be spoiled by my grandparents. I loved Danville because many of my relatives lived there and I had a large extended family of aunts, uncles and cousins to hang out and play with.

It may sound odd, but I still remember a particularly important landmark building that sits at the almost halfway point between my house and my grandparents' house. It is the beautiful Beech Grove Baptist Church located right off Highway 150 between Springfield and Perryville.

The halfway point never had any real significance on the ride there. However, I knew whenever we passed it, there was going to be a good chance I would be back within a few hours.

You could set your watch by me every time. At 8 p.m. I would get a mysterious stomachache just before I would be ready to go to bed. (I later learned it was called homesick.) I would feel it building, but would hope by entertaining myself and taking my mind off my parents and my home in Bloomfield, that it would pass and I would be able to last an entire overnight. Sometimes it did, but other times it lingered until my grandfather would have to pack me up, load my things in the car, and head to that infamous halfway point to meet my father. Then, ironically enough, I would cry the entire way home because I missed my grandfather.

There are three things that remain with me today about my visits to my grandparents:

1. My grandfather, the greatest fisherman of all time, teaching me how to troll fish in his bass boat;

2. My grandfather teaching me how to strum "Mary Had a Little Lamb" on his banjo; and

3. My grandmother making the world's most delicious pitcher of sweet tea.

Fortunately, for my grandparents and my dad, I eventually grew out of my homesick stage and was able to spend entire weekends in Danville, a town I consider to be my second hometown.

Fast forwarding to my late teens, I don't think I ever really shook that longing to be home. That nesting instinct eventually followed me throughout my college years.

I was destined to attend the University of Kentucky. While many of my friends were visiting college campuses all across the South, I was home buying everything I could that was blue and white and memorizing the UK Fight Song.

While they never questioned or debated my decision to attend UK, my parents had always hoped, in their hearts, that their alma mater, Centre College in Danville, would be my first choice. I always enjoyed hanging out at Centre's campus while visiting my relatives in Danville and it has always rated as one of the top schools (not only in Kentucky but in the U.S.) But because Danville felt so much like home, I felt a need to fly just a bit further from the family nest.

When my brother attended UK as a freshman, I knew there would be chances to spend some time visiting him and getting to know a little more about the university. I wanted a big school with big sports in a big town. Not even a full scholarship at any university could have lured me away.

My college days at UK were just what I expected, filled with meeting new people, experiencing new traditions and . . . parties. We were never lacking in finding reasons to throw a party. I had great friends and sorority sisters (shout out to the Chi Os) and everything about college was textbook perfect. Life was good.

Despite the fun, and of course, great academic learning experiences at UK, (that's for my dad who paid for my college) each summer, I would pack up all my belongings, throw them in my Ford Pinto and leave my friends in Lexington to move back home and work for the summer. My friends never understood how, after living an exciting nine months worth of college life, I could pack it all up every summer and return home to my "Mayberry." It was nothing unusual to me. I was living the best of two worlds and enjoying the perfect balance of two different lifestyles.

Growing up in a small town, I sometimes felt like we were on our own little island secluded from the rest of the world. Land lines were our only means of communication and for years, we only received three television stations. As I continued to go home on summer breaks, I saw things were changing and my town was advancing.

The idea that small towns are isolated from the world, with only limited resources and miles away from most amenities, no longer exists in most of the country. Even if Mayberry existed in today's world, I don't think Sara, the switchboard operator, would be around to patch in the calls from one person to another. Sheriff Andy Taylor would be calling his deputy Barney on his cell phone and as much as Aunt Bee liked talking with BFF (Best Friends Forever) Clara Edwards, I am sure she would be walking around with a Bluetooth in her ear.

Unless you live in a cave or on a remote island in the middle of the Pacific, there is no reason to be cut off from the rest of civilization anymore. The world of the Internet, cell phones, cable and satellite television allow our little towns to play on the field with the big boys. Lack of communication cannot be used as an excuse for not knowing any longer.

Technology has made keeping in touch a way of life in towns of all sizes.

Let's talk about the newest and coolest form of communication today, the social networking mania. I must admit that I came into the social networking thing kicking and screaming. "Social Networking." It sounded to me like an evening of speed dating. You would think these hip young techies could come up with a "cooler name" for this latest obsession.

This newest form of communication was of no interest to me at first. It was for high school and college kids, so I was told. Who had time anyway? I thought it would just be one more thing that I would have to monitor and update constantly. I was looking for ways to make my life easier, not more complicated.

I will be the first to admit it—I was wrong.

I am a rookie no more. I am a full-fledged badge-wearing member of the social networking society. And yes, I have become addicted just as I feared I would. I am proud to announce that I have a page on Facebook, LinkedIn, and I can tweet with the best of them on Twitter.

Social networking keeps you in touch with current friends and reacquaints you with old ones. You get a glimpse into the lives of people you can't see every day and can correspond with them when you want to.

Both my daughters are Facebook and Twitter masters and have hundreds of friends and followers. To be completely honest, my daughters never really wanted me to discover the world of Facebook for fear that maybe I would have too close a look inside their private lives and the lives of their friends. It was "their" world and a parent really had no place inside.

My daughters and I agreed, before I joined Facebook, that I would respect their privacy and not become one of their "friends" or even a "friend of their friends." If there was a "friend of a friend of a friend," I am sure they would have wanted me blocked from those as well. I am proud to say that we all co-exist on these sites quite well today.

It's this kind of technology that frees those of us in small towns from isolation. You can meet new friends, reconnect yourself with old ones, and update people on what's happening in your life or in your town. And getting the word out on an issue or other event is now as easy as posting it on your page. Your world is much bigger and your reach much broader. Size seems irrelevant on-line.

echnology has taken us into a world where the words, "I can't find it anywhere," no longer exists. Armed with either a computer or phone, you can pretty much get anything you want, anywhere you live. There are now options for 24/7 shopping on-line or by toll-free numbers that will have merchandise dropped at your doorstep in just a couple of days.

Before on-line shopping, we did things the old-fashioned way. We got in our cars and went to stores. Maybe once every month or two, my mom would pack my brother and me in the car and drive to Louisville to buy things that were not available at home. I can remember as a young girl getting excited about having to go to the "big city" to buy a dress for my mother or school clothes for my brother and me.

It took an hour's drive, one-way, along curvy roads to get to Louisville and its huge department stores. I loved the scenic beauty along the roadway, including the farms with acres of pasture land, farm houses, and the creeks and rivers we would pass by on our way. I loved those little towns, the ones that were even smaller than my own, that we would pass through on the way to the big city. Most of those were the "reduce-your-speed-limit-just-passing-through-on-the-way-to-somewhere-else" kind of town that I spoke of earlier.

Those of us who lived in small towns used these trips to the big city as not just a shopping trip but as a sort of day on the town. We would leave early and stay late, and try to cram as much into that day as possible. The entertainment would start immediately as we played car games like "Bee Bee Bumblebee" or "I Spy" on the hour-long trip. It was great family time together, until, or course, my brother and I would find something to fight about in the back seat and my mom would speak those five little words that made a big impact, "Don't make me pull over!" She never did, because fear made us behave.

We would arrive just when the stores would open. Our day would include shopping, going to see a movie, going out to dinner, and then stopping somewhere on the way home for ice cream. As you can see, we didn't make these trips to Louisville very often, so we would make the most of it while we were there.

I tend to be quite the traditionalist and want my girls to have some of the same opportunities I had, no matter how small and trivial they may seem today. So shopping trips like this were the norm for them growing up as well.

Living in a small town, we got used to traveling several counties away to buy clothing, go to movies, or even eat at chain restaurants. When I was younger, I thought how neat it would be to live in a big city with all these wonderful options right outside your door. Did these people go shopping every day? Did they eat out at a different restaurant every night? I was in envy of having so much, so close—something I could not imagine. What if the opposite were to happen? What about those people who have lived in the big city and moved to their own renditions of Mayberry? What kind of culture shock would they experience?

That is exactly what happened to a big city friend of mine.

As a teenager, Karen Kelling experienced summers that were the stuff of dreams. With a retired teacher as a father, her family spent their summers on the road traveling. They visited every U.S. state, Canada and Mexico. They didn't stay in luxury hotels or rent condos—they camped, either in a travel trailer or in a tent. They were able to experience nature at its best.

Karen said as a teenager she detested being dragged away from her friends and being forced to endure a summer with her parents and two sisters. But in retrospect, she loved it and would do all it again. Little did she know at the time, but one of these summer trips out west would be an introduction to an area of the country that she would eventually call home.

Karen was born and raised on the Jersey Shore, got married and lived in Farmington Hills, a suburb of Detroit, Michigan. One day her husband asked her if she would consider packing up everything and moving to Westcliffe, Colorado (Pop. 462), a small town with the allure of the Wild West, wide open spaces and spectacular views of the Sangre De Cristo Mountains. This was the total opposite of her suburban lifestyle in Michigan.

Karen recalls, "Because of the summers spent with my family in Colorado Springs, I was 110 percent in favor of the move. I loved the climate, the people and the outdoors and I longed for a lifestyle that was less hectic and materialistic." Karen and her husband initially spent only their summers in Westcliffe, planning one day to retire to its beauty. But when their son, Slade, was born in 1999, they moved up their timetable so he could grow up in Westcliffe, and not have to endure being uprooted from future friends. Six months after Slade's birth, they became full-time residents of Westcliffe.

"I love my new life. It is a widespread community that celebrates its right to privacy, yet always offers a friendly welcome or concerned interest in you." The old adage, "A man is as good as his word" rang true in every occurrence of interaction within the community. "I could count on just about anyone to come to my rescue if ever I needed help and felt indebted to do the same. It was an environment that would help my son make better choices between right and wrong."

The population of Westcliffe fluctuates from season to season because of the part-time residents who prefer one season or another. Karen describes Westcliffe as having a sense of being the last great place on earth, a hidden secret that no one wants to brag about for fear that the population will skyrocket and its uniqueness be invaded.

Karen has realized that small towns are great communities for children, but they also come with plenty of challenges including planning, which tends to be a necessity.

"You plan shopping for food, meeting people for get-togethers, or even play dates for kids." Westcliffe is not just a small town; it is a remote small town. One hour traveling time is the minimum to any urban setting that might boast a hospital or orthodontist. As far as neighbors go, "You don't have the luxury of popping in to see someone when your closest neighbor is one or two miles away."

What Karen misses most about the city is spontaneity—you can decide on a whim to go to a movie or call to have a pizza delivered. In Westcliffe, restaurant delivery is nonexistent, especially for Karen, who lives fifteen miles out of town.

As we say over and over again in this book, the small town lifestyle is not for everyone, and certainly a life in such a remote place would be challenging for those who thrive on excitement and things—things to do, things to buy, just things in general. Instead, the things you get in a life like Karen's are trust, serenity, security, morals, and community.

Moving from a big city to a small town can take getting used to. In an effort to help anyone attempting to make that move, here are a few of Karen's tips.

Karen's Tips for Survival in a Sexy Small Town

1. Keep in contact with your friends for two reasons. One, you keep in contact with the world in other aspects than what you see on the news. Two, you realize how blessed you are to live in a place where you don't have to get caught up in the craziness of the world. You can choose to enter the craziness on a temporary basis, but you can always retreat back to your comfort zone.

2. Treasure the special times that you have with your loved ones. Many may look around Westcliffe and say, "This is boring . . . there's nothing to do." Once you are into the lifestyle that IS

Westcliffe, you realize that you have been given a precious gift that eludes many . . . family time.

3. This last bit of advice harkens back to the title of an old rock tune, "Love the One You're With." Hence, you spend a lot of time with your loved ones. Without mutual love and respect for your partner and children, life could be desolate. I am happy in my relationship, so I feel secure in knowing that any temporary challenge can be overcome, because of the strong bonds of love.

*S*ome of my favorite scenes on *The Andy Griffith Show* had to do with Opie and his daily summer lifestyle. These scenes included taking off with his friends for the day, riding his bike, climbing trees, and ending up on a warm summer day at the fishin' hole. None of these activities seem extraordinary and probably, to most, not very interesting—unless activities like these were on your daily agenda while growing up.

I could relate to that laid-back lifestyle during my summers growing up in my little Mayberry part of the world.

Why is it that some of your best childhood memories are the most vivid ones? But if you were to ask me where I spent last year's vacation, it would take me a minute.

I can remember waking up in the mornings to the fragrance of the largest lilac bush you have ever seen right outside my bedroom window. The birds would be singing and the sunshine would be pouring into my window, waking me like an alarm clock. I recall just lying there, taking it all in, and knowing that the hardest decision that I would have to make that day would be deciding where my friends and I would be riding our bikes.

We never stayed in the house. We had no cable, no video games, and no iPods. The only pods we knew of were the pea pods in the garden next door.

We would ride our bikes everywhere and on every country road we could find, with no fear of encountering strangers or being abducted. We had no fear of the highway itself or the fifteen or twenty cars that would pass us by going around at fifty miles per hour. It was because of this adventurous spirit I was able to experience things, off the beaten path, and see the countryside, the creeks and the woods, and experience nature up close and personal.

This love of the outdoors led me to one of my more exotic and unusual hobbies I would develop as a kid. I was to be a 4-H entomologist for one summer. Not only would I be riding my bike all across the back roads, I would now take a butterfly net and fill my days with searching for and catching insects and butterflies. During the day, I would explore the fields and farm ponds. I would turn over rocks looking for rare bugs and beetles. At night, I would sit for hours by pole lights in the county waiting for that perfect Luna moth.

It was unfortunate for the insects that I was pretty good at this. However, it wasn't until two blue ribbons at our county and state fair, that I developed a consciousness about killing these beautiful insects. I handed over my killing jar to a fellow entomologist and retired my butterfly net.

$\mathcal{W}$e all had developed a great spirit of adventure from growing up in a small town because our choices of activities were limited. We learned to be creative in entertaining ourselves with the simplest of things to do. My friends and I would take turns playing leap-frog over the parking meters, or enjoying a game of hide-and-seek in our downtown stores, climbing over their counters and inside the clothing racks. The store owners were very tolerant of our fun and would always try to help the "hiders" in finding the most out-of-sight locations.

You have probably heard the small town joke, "My town was so boring, for fun we would watch the stoplight change." Honestly. I lived that joke. That is exactly what we would do on a Friday or Saturday night.

As sad as it may sound, some of my most enjoyable evenings were spent watching the one stoplight we had in town change colors. The traffic light was located at the only real intersection in town, which was the epicenter of the entire community. On one corner was a gas station, another a beauty shop, on the other a general store. The corner where we would sit was the one in front of Snider's Drug Store. It was the town's famous corner where you caught the school bus, waited for rides out of town and watched parades go by. At night, it was the intersection that everyone had to pass through in town to get to where they were going. We would entertain ourselves for hours watching people drive by, seeing who was with whom and taking turns guessing where they were going. I remember that I couldn't wait to start driving so I could be one of those people headed for somewhere exciting and not just having to experience it from the corner.

While I never knew it then, I grew up a bit isolated in Bloomfield. Most everything my friends and I did involved our town or sometimes the even-smaller communities around us like Chaplin and Fairfield. There was a whole other part of our rural county that I never had much of a chance to experience. It wasn't until high school that I realized that my county consisted of more than our three little communities and the "big city" of Bardstown.

There is nothing stronger in a small town than the pride the residents have in the place they call home. Who cares about that special aroma of the large cattle farm outside of town, rolling in on a warm summer day, or that many of its buildings could qualify for a month-long segment of an extreme makeover program? We all realize it's okay that your town's not perfect because it is these things that are the character and the texture of the community, and what makes it distinctive from every other town. This pride is so endearing in so many small towns across the U.S. and is quite apparent, as they post this pride for all to see in their signs and their slogans, that welcome us into their towns.

These are some examples of welcome signs and or small town slogans that proud townspeople e-mailed, blogged me, or I found on-line while writing this book:

Cambridge, Nebraska—"Life is Good"

Armour, North Dakota—"Pride Runs Deep"

Mathis, Texas—"BIG Lake, Small Town, Great People" (Pop. 5,000)

Brandon, Iowa—"Small Town We're Proud to Call Home"

Wabaunsee County, Kansas—"Small Towns, Big Opportunities"

Alexandria, Indiana—"Welcome to Small Town USA"

Dumfries, Virginia—"Small Town-Big Difference"

Wayne, Ohio—"Home to 941 Nice People and One Sorehead"

Hillsdale, Michigan—"It's the People"

Kalama, Washington—"The Small Town with Big Horizons"

Tangipahoa, Louisiana—"The Place Where Everybody is Somebody"

Acton, California—"For an Hour or a Lifetime"

New Vienna, Iowa—"The eNVy of Iowa"

Shelton, Nebraska—"A Slice of the Good Life"

Hartford, Kentucky—"Home of 2000 Happy People and a Few Soreheads"

Garrison, Texas—"Biggest Little Town in East Texas"

Williamsburg, Kentucky—"Feels Like Home"

Nashua, New Hampshire—"Best Place to Live in America"

And my personal favorite:

Hondo, Texas—"This is God's Country. Please don't drive through it like Hell."

SMALL TOWN *Sexy*

is knowing that you are more

than what people perceive you to be.

"There's a lot more business out there in small town America then I ever dreamed of."

—Sam Walton

chapter five

CAN BIG FISH
SWIM IN A SMALL POND?

*I*t seems extremely possible that when Jerome Monroe Smucker and Leon Leonwood Bean decided to start their businesses in their own small towns, that the size of the town was not the issue, it was the reason. Both gentlemen had visions of operating a successful small town business, with no idea of what was to come.

In 1897, J.M. Smucker, founder of the Smucker Company, started his jam business in the small, friendly town of Orrville, Ohio, selling his first product, apple butter, from a horse-drawn wagon with each jar carrying a personal seal of guaranteed quality. Four generations later this company produces everything from its original apple butter to health and natural foods. For more than a century, the company has made its products in their factory in the center of Orrville, which currently boasts a population of 8,551.

You may not know him by his first or middle name, but you certainly know him by his initials. Leon Leonard Bean, the founder of one of the most popular outdoor sporting and clothing goods companies, started his business, L.L. Bean, in Freeport, Maine, in 1912. After starting small, as just a rubber boot company, L.L. Bean added to its inventory and became famous as a mail-order catalog company, still headquartering itself in Freeport. The company, almost 100 years later, is now a true focal point of this small town (Pop. 7,800) with its retail store and many other outdoor features for visitors as well as residents.

Both Smucker and Bean realized that the size of your town truly did not matter when you have a vision and a desire to do something great. These men are both testaments to the statement, "Yes, big fish can swim in small ponds."

There are many more small town visionary success stories just like these with companies we have all heard of, like Cracker Barrel, in Lebanon, Tennessee; Tabasco on tiny Avery Island, just over 100 miles west of New Orleans; and of course, giant discount retailer Wal-Mart, born in Bentonville, Arkansas. In our area of central Kentucky, those brilliant minds that discovered the world of bourbon making knew that their small towns were the only places they wanted to produce their American native spirit. What each of these companies has in common is the fact that their products were born in these small American towns of less than 15,000 people.

Most of these companies are deeply rooted in their communities, and their towns carry a great deal of pride because that company is there. Historically, these companies tend to be an anchor in the community and are the largest employer, as well as among the most philanthropic in civic activities. It is companies and corporations like these in small towns that help build community and civic centers, donate to sports teams and venues, and help non-profit organizations survive.

Of course, doing business in small town America has come a long way since Mr. Smucker or Mr. Bean thought that selling one product might help them pay their bills. As I have said before, technology has changed not only our personal lives, but the way we do business. While small towns were an appealing place to start a small business in the early 1900s, any obstacle they may have faced about becoming national or marketing their product globally no longer exists.

*C*raig White couldn't wait to get out of his small Alabama town when he was growing up. Everyone there walked to work at the cotton mill every day, and he knew he needed a bigger city with bigger opportunities.

Now, years later, the senior vice president for Flowers Bakeries admits that he is now back where he never thought he would be, in a small town. However, this time, it is his choice and he says, it is exactly where he wants to be.

Flowers Foods' corporate headquarters is located in the beautiful south Georgia town of Thomasville, (Pop. 19,000). Located near the Florida border, Thomasville touts itself as a Georgia paradise where the air is clean, the people are friendly and traffic jams are unheard of. *U.S. News and World Report* once touted Thomasville as "amenity rich for its small size."

When the Flowers Foods Company started looking at locations for their newest state-of-the-art baking facility in the U.S., they were originally looking at an area in Northern Kentucky. The towns were larger and had more of a metropolitan feel because where one town ended the other began and there seemed to be little green space to separate the towns. White went to the company's chairman of the board and said while he liked that area, he thought the company should be located somewhere else, somewhere that would better match up with the company's culture.

White said, "Of course in the end, economics, what one city is willing to do over another, does play a role in where you are going to locate a company, but honestly, that is a small part of it. Bottom line, it comes down to the community and its culture. For us, with this bakery, the logistics and what kind of road accessibility you have were critically important to the freshness of our product and Bardstown, Kentucky, fits best for what were looking for in our newest bakery."

White added, "Interstates 65, 64 and 75 are all in close proximity to Bardstown and the town's small-town way of life played a big role in the final site selection decision because it was in line in Flowers Foods' culture and where we began. We want to be in a town where you can still see someone walking down the street and you know who it is."

"When we choose where we want to be, it must lend itself to what company founders W. H. and L. S. Flowers taught us, and that is 'don't get away from your culture.' I still believe that rural America is what made this country what it is and is the backbone of this country and you find the working people who still care. That is what Flowers is looking for."

Less than two years after their very first visit to Bardstown, I was there with local and state dignitaries, including Kentucky governor Steve Beshear, when we officially celebrated the opening of the Bardstown Flowers Foods facility. Flowers Foods rolled their first loaves of bread off the lines in their new facility in the Nelson County Industrial Park. It was a huge day for Flowers, but an even bigger day for Bardstown.

Thirty years ago, very few small towns across the country would have even been considered as a location for a big company like Flowers. There has been a sort of evolution process for many towns that decided they wanted to get serious about bringing big business to small town America. It has taken great leaders, like former Bardstown Mayor Gus Wilson, who realized to grow a community, you must adjust your way of thinking to be competitive. In those days, that meant providing the infrastructure necessary to do big business. In our town, it meant buying land for industrial purposes, and providing water, electric, sewer and natural gas to this land, to have it ready for that first great industrial client. Today, decades later, we continue to reap the benefits of this foresight, and Flowers Foods continues to be proof that if you build it, they might just come.

*T*ake a look around. It's not your grandmother's small town anymore. Small towns have to become competitive in economic development because so many small towns have now jumped into the business of recruiting companies. Small towns are turning tobacco fields into industrial parks and extending utilities into rural areas in hopes that a company may decide to do business there.

Thirty years ago, companies wouldn't look at a location that didn't have water or electric; now, one of the bare basics for recruiting is high speed Internet accessibility. It doesn't come cheap. Communities are spending millions of dollars to make sure they keep up with the latest in technology.

The Internet is transforming small town entrepreneurs and businesses and extending their reach for customers. Some of these businesses that understand the importance of being "wired" are now extending their reach of operations not only nationally, but globally.

What's so great about today's wired world?

Today, to do multi-million dollar deals, you don't have to be located on the 76th floor of a glass office tower in a metropolitan area. Cyber commuting allows us do the same deal from offices on Main Street, USA or even from your home's dining room table. Even better, the client will never know the difference.

A good website is like having a great office building and visible sign. Where we were using our office addresses and telephone numbers before, we are now relying on our website and e-mail addresses to correspond with our clients.

There are so many smart small towns out there that "get it." Their leaders understand the need for this technology and are marching forward with an attitude of getting wired and providing aggressive IT options for their residents and businesses.

Believe me, small towns have their share of frustration and challenges. Because of physical limitations and little or no budgets, there are still so many towns lacking the necessary technology to move ahead to promote any sort of e-trade for their local businesses. Unfortunately, these are some of the towns that are declining in population because companies cannot grow and compete, and that limited access to the world is a detriment to anyone thinking about moving to these small towns.

Having your town wired has become one of our infrastructure necessities of the century. It is as important as water, sewage and phone service and influences our decisions on where we choose to live and where companies chose to locate. It was not that long ago that the Internet was a luxury and only something you could get if you lived or worked in the big cities.

"Times are a-changing" is something my grandfather would always say to me. I never understood then what he meant and would always just smile and shake my head. But I get it now, almost forty years later.

If you are reading this book, waiting for your dial-up to connect, you need to go shake up your local leaders and drag them into the 21st century of technology. We need to listen to our young generation because they are the ones who can hold our hands and lead us into this wonderful world of technology. And if talking techie stuff makes absolutely no sense to you, go find a teenager and hire them to tutor you in the language of today. If not, that cyber train is taking off and you are not going to be on it.

This insight allows small towns to compete, not just with counties surrounding them, but with other communities in other states in the U.S. Many have risen to the level of competition on an international level. Towns, like Bardstown, no longer only compete with communities in my state, but Bardstown is competing with towns in states all over the country. It is not uncommon for a client to say he has narrowed his search to three states, and Kentucky is one, and your community is one of the four being considered in this state alone.

*I*n the 1980s, the U.S. experienced a series of events that changed the landscape of many of its small towns in the Southern U.S. It was the influx of the auto industry, with several major automakers locating in the South, including Nissan and Saturn in Tennessee and Toyota Motor Manufacturing in Kentucky.

In December of 1985, an announcement was made that is still considered today to be one of the most important in economic development history in the Commonwealth of Kentucky. Toyota would build its largest manufacturing facility outside of Japan in the

Commonwealth of Kentucky. Not only would this automotive giant be locating in our state, but in the small town of Georgetown, Kentucky (population at that time was around 11,000). In this global marketplace, with every state rolling the red carpet out for companies like this, they choose a small town. Apparently, the Japanese automakers understood the meaning of *Small Town Sexy*.

At the time, Gov. Martha Layne Collins and her economic development staff, including Executive Cabinet Secretary and Budget Director Larry Hayes, knew this would be something big. Something so big, that it would change communities all across the state. New buildings would be constructed, good paying jobs would be created, and the tax bases for these towns and counties would increase significantly. The 1980s and 1990s were boom years for numerous communities in Kentucky.

But why did Toyota choose the small town of Georgetown, Kentucky? Governor Collins remembered this time as one of the most exciting in her governmental career and vividly recalls the intense competition for this project. "There were twenty states competing for the Toyota project, and there was a combination of requirements that the company had, including rail, a major highway, and a large parcel of land. Being in a metropolitan area was not a requirement because the Japanese loved wide-open spaces and ample green space. As long as a larger city was nearby, like Lexington, with airline service and other amenities, then other needs could be met."

Of course, factors outside of livability issues played into their decision as well, including a smartly-designed incentive package from the state. But if you know the Japanese way of life, it is important for them to live and work in a place that is a right fit for their work ethic and culture.

What Governor Collins won't tell you is that they just liked us here in Kentucky. While she is far too humble to accept any credit, many will tell you it was her savvy demeanor combined with her staff's astute business sense that helped win Toyota over.

Toyota economically changed Georgetown forever. The population went from 11,000 to 21,000 in only seventeen years. If you do the math, you will understand that's a heck of an increase in such a short time and a true economic boom for that community.

Not only was the town of Georgetown changed forever, but dozens of small towns all across the South were changed as automotive suppliers of all sizes followed these plants and moved within an easy drive of the facility. Hundreds of Japanese would be moving into these areas and integrating their families into a new American lifestyle as well as sharing their culture with new friends and neighbors.

Bardstown is home to several Japanese companies including our most recent, NPR Manufacturing. NPR (Nippon Piston Ring) is one of the few producers of piston rings in the world, and I worked with their company officials to help convince them that Bardstown would be the perfect location for their new U.S. facility.

During this process, from the first day they arrived in Bardstown in 2006 to the last "Kanpai" with sake, toasting the official start up, I became good friends with the company's president, Yasuyoshi Egami. He loved our small town, and we loved having him here and learning about his culture and his life in Japan. NPR chose Bardstown from about fifty sites they were looking at across the country and in Mexico. Bardstown stood out because of the close proximity to their customers, Toyota, Honda, Nissan and GM. You can be at most of those locations within a day's drive. They also discovered that a lot of Japanese companies were advancing and succeeding in our small town and that our governmental leaders were inviting and understanding of Japanese people.

It would be a big change of lifestyle for Egami, who was a big city Japanese executive. In Japan, he and his family lived in downtown Tokyo, one of the largest cities in the world. An engineer by trade, Egami designed and built his own home amongst the skyscrapers. I always found it so fascinating that he was living two extremely different lifestyles. When he returned to Japan on frequent visits, he would be in the fast-paced, big-city world, taking trains and experiencing long commutes. Then, in Bardstown, he would basically be back to the country, with nature all around and just a short distance from work.

In Japan, Egami's daily commute was over an hour to work on the train and another hour back. So you can imagine his thrill when he drove to the office in less than ten minutes. Another perk of living in Bardstown was the golf, a favorite pastime of his. It's not only very expensive to play golf in Tokyo, about $200 per round, but you typically do not play in a natural setting. Most courses are located within a city and it sometimes takes him two hours to get to a course. In Bardstown, he was literally able to walk out his front door and be on the fairway, since he lived in one of the several golf course communities in town.

He grew to love our Southern food but also found true Japanese cuisine only about thirty minutes away. If you know anything about the Japanese, most love American bourbon. Egami enjoyed bragging to his friends in Japan that he was living in the "Bourbon Capital of the World" and always made sure to return to Japan with gifts on his visits home.

After two years in the U.S. and the successful start-up of a new company, Egami has moved back to Japan. He told me recently that it's not the golf or the bourbon he misses most about his Kentucky home, but the employees he trained and who started his company's new Kentucky venture.

From our first encounter, Egami and I became instant friends. It wasn't hard convincing him that he would find his life in small town America quite enjoyable. And he did. He enjoyed everything our small town had to offer, and soon was a stranger no more.

In September of 2007, I eagerly accepted an invitation from Egami and his company to visit their corporate office in Tokyo and their two manufacturing facilities in northern Japan. Small town girl meets one of the largest cities in the world. Talk about a fish out of water, this little guppy had just been thrown into the Pacific Ocean for a week-long swim.

My seven-day trip to Japan could be a book all its own, an adventure that was nothing less than an amazing experience, full of learning a new culture and traditions, getting an up-close look at Japanese business, experiencing their technology, and the food, that incredible Japanese cuisine. I promised I would taste it all, and I did.

After my visit to Japan I realized one of the reasons why the Japanese enjoy the small town culture that exists in Kentucky. It's because of the genuine respect that we have for each other. The respect they showed me while visiting their country is so much like our well-known Southern hospitality, just in a different language.

$\mathscr{W}$hat is the international allure of small towns? Outside of the people and places, what is it that makes small towns alluring to companies that have no relationship to the area at all?

To answer this puzzling question, I went to an expert, a gentleman who not only helps locate Japanese companies to the South, but who also finds the right executives to work and live in large cities or small towns.

Andy Ito is an executive search and management consultant with Win Advisory Group in Nashville, Tennessee.

Born and raised in Sapporo, the fourth largest city in Japan, he has lived in the U.S. for the past twenty years.

To speak with Andy you would think he has lived here all his life. His English is as good as anyone born in the U.S. and he is very stylish in the way of American fashion. He is one of those guys who could fit in perfectly in downtown Manhattan or Franklin, Kentucky. Growing up in Japan, he had American influences, including owning a 1973 Mustang Grande and eating at fast food chains like McDonald's and Kentucky Fried Chicken.

Andy and I hit it off the first time he brought a client to my town. He is a big fan of Bardstown.

By this time, you have probably learned this truism about me: "To like my town is to like me." Andy's compliments of my town made me an instant fan.

Speaking from experience, because he has so many clients in small Southern towns, he realized in the last few years that the stereotypes so many of us face in our small towns seem to be fading. His clients are now recognizing the appeal of small towns.

"As an international recruiter, there is that tendency to believe that it's difficult to find qualified professionals in a small town. Whether it's true to not, in this sense, the clients in small towns will be potential targets for recruiters like us. And also, from a candidate standpoint, small towns are no longer places with less opportunity."

Halleluiah! These are words that every economic developer in small towns all across the country has been waiting to hear. While we have been telling clients this for years, it doesn't really resonate until an "outsider" explains the reasons.

Andy says that he has seen a shift in the last decade—manufacturing facilities among global corporations are staying away from suburban and metropolitan areas for reasons like higher labor costs, more regulatory and compliance issues, unionized activities and higher turnover. On the executives' personal side of the equation, they are seeking a good quality of life for themselves and their families. The good traditional charm of small towns is the perfect alternative for those with heightened consciousness for lifestyle and family.

This was not always the case. More than ten years ago, most Japanese expatriates stationed in small towns all across the country were commonly saying, "There is nothing to do in this town." More recently, however, they seem to have been shifting toward comfort, safety (less crime), stability, and relationships. It is these unchanged consistent factors that make Japanese executives feel very comfortable about living and doing business in small towns.

Small towns that are near "things to do" are often going to have a leg up on their competition. Andy has learned that being close to places that have a variety of ethnic restaurants and the arts and cultural activities will help to keep a client happy and sustain them over the years.

Andy said the allure of small town areas is so high that he has clients willing to take a significantly lower income to live in these towns. He also told me about a Japanese sales management executive who jumped at the chance to relocate his family from Chicago to small town America. Later, he admitted that the executive had actually located to my hometown.

Halleluiah again!

Let's revisit what I have said before and will echo a couple times again.

Not every international client or executive is going to want small town America. Whether they have grown accustomed to a big city lifestyle, or have the impression that you cannot live and do big business in a small town, it's important to stress that small towns are not for everyone. That's okay. If we were, everyone would be moving here and small town America would no longer exist as we appreciate it today.

⌒⌒

*I*nternationally, what is the *Small Town Sexy* allure? What brings people thousands of miles and across oceans, to locate not in New York City, Los Angeles or Chicago, but in small communities they have, more than likely, never heard of?

Everyone has a different story: they were relocated by a company, brought over the border for construction jobs, followed a family member that moved here on business, or just came on their own, because they wanted to experience the lifestyle they had heard so much about.

Roger Dalraine is one of my favorite international "brought-ins." Born and raised in the U.K., Roger speaks with a beautiful accent. As a successful entrepreneur, he always has something to teach me in our conversations. Like my other favorite British character, James Bond, Roger is often covert; however, we have spoken on many occasions about some of his projects including international technology and security. He has lived in communities of all sizes in many different countries but he prefers the life that small towns offer.

Roger says doing business in small towns is surprisingly easier than most would think. "Technology is readily available at home or at various hot spots in town, our state-of-the-art library has resources I use quite often and an international airport is only forty minutes from my home."

When he is not doing business, you can find Roger and his wife, Estelle, enjoying their community as much, if not more, than anyone born and raised here. They have become some our best volunteers. They have taken a couple of our most visited sites, the One Room Log School House just off Court Square and Veterans Memorial Park, and worked their green thumb magic to turn them into areas of pride for the community. No recognition needed—they do it because they want to and because they care.

When a fresh perspective is needed about what makes life in a small town so appealing, ask someone like Roger who was not born there. Roger has his "why I love small towns" list. It includes enjoying the quaint non-franchised restaurants and pubs, and the Farmer's Markets where you can get fresh fruits and vegetables from the farmers who grew them. He appreciates the good service from the local shop owners who not only know you by name, but how you like your coffee. Roger's reason that makes me most proud is that our children and teenagers are very polite and invariably friendly and helpful.

The Dalraines are not alone in their newfound love of small town America. The Zarbs, a family of wonderful Australian musicians, are some of our more visible international "brought-ins" in Bardstown. After living here for several years, they decided they wanted to give back to their new community by hosting a concert to introduce us to Australian music.

This cross-cultural event now takes place every year around the Fourth of July holiday. We close the main thoroughfare in town for a stage with the Historic Old Courthouse as a natural backdrop. People bring lawn chairs, sit back, and enjoy the music late into the evening.

ith international residents, come other worldly options. Fifteen years ago, you would be hard pressed to find many ethnic restaurants in small towns, but now our children are growing up with more dining choices than ever before. Japanese, Chinese and Korean cuisine is now offered by our Asian neighbors, and most communities have at least one Mexican restaurant being operated by local Hispanic families.

In Bardstown, we also have a restaurant owned and operated by a Bosnian couple, who were refugees brought to the area to escape the war. Merima and Dzevad Kreso renovated an old downtown movie theatre into an elegant international restaurant and conference facility. Their future project will include another building renovation for an Italian restaurant.

Lebanon, Kentucky (Pop. 5,931), has also been very successful in their economic development efforts due to the growing global economy.

Many Japanese companies have chosen this central Kentucky town as their home.

To celebrate these new residents, people from all over the region attend the annual Marion County Japanese Cultural Day. This event has grown in popularity over the years and allows the Japanese families who have moved into the area a chance to share the culture and traditions of their country with their new community.

I used to think that as an economic developer I needed two different "bags of tricks" for my recruiting efforts: one for companies looking for a place to locate and one for families looking for a new community to live. However, I have discovered, that the factors that entice people to small towns are the same factors that bring companies. Good schools, affordable cost of living, good workers, religious options, and a sense of community are among the most popular reasons.

Kudos to those towns that have successfully lured big companies to their area. They employ large numbers of local residents and their economic impact on the community is significant. However, as I have said before, not all small towns are primed to be the home of big business.

That's okay, because for decades, communities have been surviving on the successes of another type of business: home-grown entrepreneurs. Sometimes you only have to look as far as your own backyard to find those successful entrepreneurs and good business minds who don't want to work for large companies, but want to be their own boss.

Just like towns, small business owners often do not get the respect they deserve because of their size. They may not employ a large number of people and they are not always able to make large contributions to various community causes. But don't let their individual size fool you. Together, they are strong in numbers. Think about any small town you know. What are the businesses that line the downtown and any other of the outlying shopping areas? They are small businesses, often employing less than ten people. In any small town, it's these small businesses that keep the heart of the community pumping.

Just think about some of the small businesses in your town that you depend on every day. It's early afternoon and already today, I have been to the convenience store, the coffee shop, the dry cleaner, a downtown retailer, my dentist, and the drug store. I bet your days are similar.

Dreams don't always have to be big. Getting sound advice from people who have gone down this road before is a first step to being successful in a small town. Rely on your local Chamber of Commerce for resource information, your local community college, and Small Business Development Centers. Don't forget about small town banks that have an interest in seeing the community grow. Working with these groups are your first best steps in fulfilling your dream of owning your own business. You never know, you may be the next J.M Smucker or L.L. Bean.

Okay, we have talked about big business, international business, and small business, so what else is there to talk about in making your small town successful?

SHOP LOCAL! These are two little words that carry a big message. Small town business owners have dedicated themselves to being part of the community by offering a service or product, and to be successful they need your support. Pass the word and spend your money where your home and heart are, and with the people who live down the street or you see at church on Sunday.

To survive the current economic environment, small towns must move forward in significant ways. Baby steps are no longer an option. Towns must invest in technology as well as other infrastructure if they want to compete—while at the same time not losing sight of the small town charm that has made them appealing. Is this possible? Of course it is. Just ask the mayors of Orrville, Ohio; Freeport, Maine; or even Thomasville, Georgia. Their communities continue to co-exist nicely with companies like Smuckers, L.L. Bean and Flowers Foods.

SMALL TOWN *Sexy*

is knowing that the best of ideas

usually start small and sometimes in small places.

"Fame is only good for one thing—
they will cash your check in a small town."
—Truman Capote

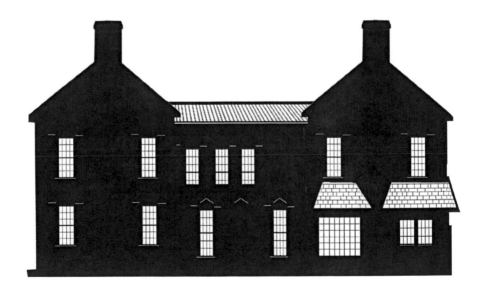

chapter six

"PARADE IT" FOR ALL TO SEE

*N*obody throws a party better than people in a small town. I can say that with all the confidence and experience to back it up. As long as I have been able to walk, I've had my hand in some stage of planning a festival, parade, or other event in the community.

It doesn't take much for us to want to throw a party—and we can find the darndest things to celebrate.

It's time you took a little break from reading because I have a short exercise for you. I want you to put down the book, close your eyes, and think about the festivals or special events that you have attended in any small town. If you haven't been to one, don't open your eyes yet, because I want you to imagine what you think one would look like. (Pause for mental rewind of your life.)

For those of us who have been fortunate enough to visit a festival, there are usually very vivid images in our minds associated with them. Think about the time of year it was, who was there, your age, and the kind of festival. What did you eat? Did you ride any rides? Did you have fun? Okay, do you have that image in your mind—so vividly you can almost taste the funnel cake and hear the calliope on the merry-go-round? If so, then I bet you also have a big smile on your face remembering a good time and a good place.

It's these simple times in our life that make lasting memories. Although we might not remember what we had for breakfast this morning, we do have these wonderfully nostalgic events in our lives that occurred, maybe decades ago. This is *Small Town Sexy* at its best!

I have many favorite memories of festivals, but a couple really stand out.

Remember my hometown of Bloomfield was best known as being the home of the Bloomfield Tobacco Festival. Bloomfield would double its population for those few days in October when visitors from all across the state would arrive to take part in the fun. For days before the event, we would decorate floats for the parade through downtown; for weeks, festival organizers would go to church and pray for the best weather. However, we are from Kentucky, where we realize weather is always an uncertainty, even in October. For the locals, the festival was a homecoming, where those who moved away, would return to visit family and use this time as a reunion with friends.

My family always had a role to play in the festival, from making floats and working the booths, to serving on some sort of committee. No matter what was going on that month, everything else was put on hold. This was always a family affair. No one planned weddings, the birth of a baby and—heaven forbid—that anyone would pass away that week.

*J*am a festival magnet. Festivals find me when I least expect them and uncontrollably pull me in. I will happen upon parades on my vacation travels and force everyone with me out of the car to watch it go by. I will show up for a conference when a major festival is taking place in that city and instigate a group to play hooky to experience the flavor of the event. I once happened upon the Puerto Rican Day Parade in downtown New York City as I was attempting to locate our hotel with my daughters. After circling the same block for over an hour trying to find a street that was not closed, we gave in, parked the car, and joined the thousands of onlookers lining the parade route. I have randomly come upon a Pumpkin Festival in Allardt, Tennessee, where I browsed aisle after aisle of booths, and danced for hours at a Firemen's Street event in Jerome, Arizona. Music festivals in Telluride, Colorado, and Lebanon, Ohio, to a Spring Celebration in Madison, Indiana entertained me for days with their great concerts and performers.

It was a real treat to enjoy another community's event, without having to help in organizing. The only thing for me to do was have fun. This felt good—real good. Although my inner festival planner did not leave entirely—I found myself at each of these events counting the number of Port-a-Johns they rented. Once a planner, always a planner.

Like Paula Deen knows her way around a kitchen, I know my way around a festival.

My festival résumé is long. It includes everything from the sitting around a table with friends and determining the next great festival idea to the picking up trash when it's over. Don't try to have any intelligent conversation with a festival organizer the week of an event. Anything other than "the event" doesn't matter. We don't sleep because we worry about the weather and our brains are forcing us to multi-task at super-human levels. It's called being in "festival mode" and no one must break our concentration.

I have blistered my fingers stuffing chicken wire to make a hay wagon look like a flag and spent hours chalking the float line-up area, only to have heavy rain wash the numbers away. I have ridden on floats and served as a judge for floats. I have even helped Santa, after he lost his britches in front of the marching band, get them back on, pinned and back on his sleigh. But my friends and family will tell you my most amazing feat is how I con them into taking on a role in each of the events that I plan.

I use my "having a baby" analogy on them. I tell them, "Yes, guys, we will have to put in some long, hard months and toward the end it will be painful. Trust me, when it all comes together and people tell you how great it was, I promise that you will forget about the pain and won't want to wait until next year to do it again." They fall for it every time.

One of the highest parade honors you can get is being asked to emcee the event. Well, maybe the Grand Marshal is one step up, since you get to ride in a sexy convertible and do nothing more than wave at people and throw candy. Okay, emceeing is the second highest honor and one that shows you have reached a certain celebrity status.

I have been the voice of both the Bloomfield Tobacco Festival Parade and Nelson County Christmas Parade. During my television years, I did a sort of "play-by-play" as we recorded a broadcast of the Christmas parade to be played back that next week. Some valuable advice I will give to you future parade commentators: have good notes and a sidekick/color commentator with a good sense of humor.

One year, I invited my good friend Debbie Ables to help me in the play-by-play of our community Christmas Parade. Debbie is probably the most entertaining person I know, so between the two of us, with my knowledge of parades and broadcasting and her colorful and witty commentary, I knew this would be a great parade broadcast ranking up there with the likes of Macy's Thanksgiving Day parades emceed by NBC's Matt Lauer and Al Roker.

Our Christmas Parade is held at night, and it seems that it is usually the coldest night of the year. This night wasn't any different. We were bundled up like children going sleigh riding and were almost unrecognizable. We had our notes, had studied them in advance, and were ready to go. It should be easy, we thought, as each entry would have a number displayed on the front to designate who it was. The hardest part at first was manipulating our notes in mittens.

It started well. The National Guard Color Guard, the mayor in a convertible, and Miss Nelson County Fair all appeared in order, just as our notes said. Then, all of a sudden, there were floats—beautiful floats, but none had numbers. We scrambled through our notes trying to figure out which was which, as groups of unidentifiable marching school kids were in front of us and unknown dignitaries were waving in the next car. The identifying numbers had disappeared and any visible signage they had was too far away and small for us to read. We were going to have to wing it.

Fortunately, I was able to find someone on a few of the floats I knew and by process of elimination could figure out the float. However, Debbie, as someone who had not lived here all her life and didn't know these people, was forced to have to follow my lead. As you can imagine, it wasn't pretty.

I knew we were in trouble when I turned to Debbie and said, "Look at this float coming up the street. Debbie, that is certainly in the Christmas spirit of things, don't you think?"

She starred sharply at the float for few seconds and turned directly into the camera and said, "Isn't that precious?"

Precious? She did not just say "precious?"

Isn't precious a term reserved for use when talking about a sleeping newborn? Not exactly the word I would use for a group of kids wrapped up to look like Christmas boxes. But okay. Precious. Let's move on.

As the parade continued and the next float was coming our way, I could see Debbie really eyeing this one. She apparently had a thought about this one, so I turned to her with the microphone and said, "So, Debbie, it looks as if this one is apparently a favorite with you. Tell us about it."

"Well, Kim," she said. "It's just precious."

I don't really know how many seconds of dead air there had to have been, because after being a bit startled with her reply, I realized that we were still on the air and people were waiting for a response. I had none.

It was at this time that Debbie and I just looked at each other with these "reindeer in the headlight eyes" and just burst out laughing. We knew we were not going to win any award for this broadcast and to pull off the rest of the event without crying, we were going to have fun from then on out. And we did.

Now that the pressure was off, and we weren't taking ourselves so seriously, we got the hang of it after awhile. The word "precious" was never spoken again.

But . . . then came the cars—the endless line of the Whiskey City Cruisers. With the exception of Santa Claus, the Cruisers, a local group of classic car enthusiasts, were everyone's favorite entries in the parade.

These beautifully restored cars and trucks are invited to participate in events all across the state and draw a huge crowd whenever they are on display.

So, here they roll down the parade route lined up bumper to bumper as far as you could see. I thought to myself, "Okay, we have no notes on these anymore, we have about thirty cars to talk about, so how were we going to get through this?" I knew Debbie was familiar with this group because she had many friends who were Cruisers, so I was going to let her pilot the plane on this one.

"Okay, Debbie, I know you are really familiar with these guys so I think you should start us out and tell us about these cars."

Two to three cars passed, and it all went well. She knew the types of cars, Corvettes, Camaros, Thunderbirds and Mustangs. We both had grown up with these cars, so we each would spend time describing the vehicle and relating it to a story that one of us had with that particular car. For some reason, most stories seemed to center around old boyfriends.

But by car number fifteen, we had run out of things to say and were, once again, stumbling to find new words to describe these beautiful vehicles. Okay, cue colorful and entertaining Debbie. If nothing else, she would make us laugh.

"Debbie, tell us about this next beautiful red car." It was an older car, one I was not familiar with.

"Well, Kim, it's red. And what a pretty, red car. And look at that shiny chrome."

Again, I had no words. I was at a panic point, because, honestly, that's just about all I knew about that car myself. It's red and it's shiny.

Okay, I let that one pass.

Parade officials must have told the Cruisers to speed up a bit, to keep the parade going at a good pace, because the cars started coming a bit faster and sometimes two at a time.

At that point, my mind wandered to one of my favorite *I Love Lucy* television episodes where she and Ethel were working on the candy factory assembly line. Everything was going so well at first, until they sped up the conveyor belt and everything went to hell.

That was Debbie and me.

"Debbie, they're coming a little faster now, tell us about these two beautiful cars. And what about those next three or four?" I asked while frantically looking through the crowd for a possible avid car lover whom I could coax to the reviewing stand to help us out. We were ready to pay good money for a little intelligent car knowledge.

"Kim, isn't that the shiniest chrome you have ever seen?"

Oh, dear God! She said it again.

She had the same look of panic in her eyes, as I did, because she knew, also, we were once again in trouble. However, for some reason, this wave of calm suddenly fell upon both of us, and once again we both just burst into laughter. It was at this time, we both realized, it was just a parade, a wonderful small town parade. People were not going to worry about what we said, they were interested in seeing their children, their grandchildren, their friends and neighbors, walking and riding in the parade. They could just turn down the volume, tune us out, and enjoy it just the same.

Fortunately for us, the Santa float (always the last in the parade) was in our sights now and we were nearing the end. We needed no notes to talk about Santa.

For the same reason people "rubberneck" at a car wreck, we decided to watch the re-broadcast of the parade later that week to see just how bad it really was. Was it a *Small Town Sexy* broadcast? Probably not, but it was extremely entertaining. We consumed several glasses of wine during the re-broadcast, and laughed until we cried.

*P*eople who are not involved in putting on a festival or special event probably wonder why we devote so much time and energy doing this. What's the big deal? It's just an event.

To answer that question, as I have on several occasions, festivals and events are meant to spotlight and bring attention to your community, and to celebrate the sometimes eclectic reasons for that festival, whether it be bourbon, headless chickens, ham or mosquitoes. And yes, there's a festival named for each of them, as you will see shortly.

In Bardstown, we have over thirty-five festivals and events. Are we crazy? Probably. Do people come? Absolutely—they come for each and every one of them.

We have so many that we publish a brochure of all the annual events, and it's one of the most "picked up" and utilized pieces of literature we distribute. Of course, locals use them as much as visitors, so they can invite out-of-town friends and family in to join in on the fun. The events may be as small as the Annual Tour of Gardens or as large as our Kentucky Bourbon Festival, where over 50,000 people from all over the world attend a week-long event. And if you don't drink bourbon, that is no problem. There are activities for all ages and food and drink for all taste buds. While bourbon is consumed at the various events, the allure is celebrating the history of the product and watching how it is made.

While the larger, sexier festivals get most of the attention, it is sometimes the smaller ones that have a special uniqueness. These are typically a one-of-a-kind festival that is intended for a certain audience. They don't have a large theme, or a big budget. They are often a sort of "homecoming" for friends and family. This is exactly how Buttermilk Days in Bardstown was born.

Buttermilk is an African-American neighborhood just south of the Courthouse Square, and it's where the "Buttermilk Gang" originated. Not a gang like you would think about in the big city, but a gang of buddies who were born and raised together and who decided to host a cookout to celebrate their roots in that neighborhood. The original Buttermilk Gang included the Sheckles boys, Bill, Joey and Mark; Kenny Linton; Gator Tonge; Mike Lydian; Joe Dodson; and Kevin and Wayne Rogers.

It was a simple gathering at first—just an elaborate backyard bar-b-que with friends and family members. But word got out and it grew.

After four years the cookout grew to 400 people. The fifth year was a year that would change the festival forever.

A local farmer had a bad year selling hogs and told the "gang" he would give them six hogs if they wanted to have them processed to cook for the festival. With all this pork on their hands by way of sausage, bacon, chops and ribs, they thought they should have a big breakfast as well as a huge afternoon cookout. The women were in charge of all the delicious side dishes that were served. The word spread quickly: all the food you wanted and all free. Everyone came. There was music, a street dance and all the conversation you could ever want from every generation. And it was an election year, so as you can imagine, every politician within twenty-five miles was there shaking hands and kissing babies. The breakfast that first year served 250 people. Last year, around 900 were served.

Today, the event goes on for three days. It is not only highlighted by all the wonderful food, and the homemade wine tasting competition—but the wild meat cookout is a favorite night for the local hunters. It was estimated around 3,000 people attended the 2008 Buttermilk Days Festival—a festival that grew from an elaborate cookout.

This festival is one of the most popular in the area because of the fellowship from a shared heritage that goes back more than a century. Families host their reunions during this weekend and everyone else clears their schedules. Roads are closed to handle the crowds of people.

One of the oldest co-founders of Buttermilk Days is Joe Dodson. This seventy-four-year-old left Bardstown for college and the military but found his way back after living in a fast-paced area of Washington State. Dodson says this festival is about coming home and welcoming those who have been away. "It's about celebrating our heritage in this part of town and welcoming those who are not from here. By the time you leave, you are part of our Buttermilk family."

Co-founder Bill Sheckles agrees with Dodson and says there's nothing like this around. "People look forward to this all summer and can't wait for the fourth weekend in August," he says. Sheckles, who is also a city councilman for the community, says events like this are successful in small towns because people get involved and want to make a difference. He agrees that it is not unlike being involved on the city council and part of the decision-making process for the community. "People want to be part of this and want to see it do well and grow. So they get involved and they take it seriously. They may not do anything else the rest of the year, but you know you can count on them to make a contribution to the festival," Sheckles says.

Buttermilk Days is one of those events that is hard to do justice to on paper. You just have to experience this small town homecoming event. But come hungry, because you will have the opportunity to eat some of the most delicious, and sometimes most exotic, food around.

*F*estivals are for fun! They tend to be seasonal events that celebrate unique aspects of a community and often involve culture, entertainment, food, and traditions.

I have told my small town friends that I can compare a town preparing for an event or festival to that of a girl getting ready for her first prom. While she is pretty every day, for this one-time-a-year special evening, she fixes herself up like never before and looks her best for all to see. Knowing that old friends and family will be returning, new visitors will be stopping by, and that locals will be coming out to celebrate "their day," the city is spruced up and looking its best for the "party." We clean our streets, paint our curbs, plant more flowers, and make sure our welcome signs are visible for all to see.

Anyone or any community can put on a festival. If you are doing it to spotlight your community, great! If you are doing it to raise money, good luck. Have you ever priced Port-a-Johns or tents? Some festivals can make money, but most are designed as non-profit events that usually are break-even ventures. It's not about the money; it's about the experience.

Many communities and organizations are fortunate to get government or corporate sponsors to offset the costs, but even with these funds, you usually make enough to pay your bills and have enough left over to get started the next year.

Don't let that stop you. What festivals and events do accomplish is to increase the town's population during these days and hopefully increase business at gas stations, local shops, restaurants, motels and campgrounds. More importantly, it brings a community together, focused on one project and working to make it happen. It doesn't matter what school you attend, what religion you are, or what your political affiliation is, these types of festivities have everyone working together, on the same team, to make an event successful for the benefit of the town.

Not every town has or even wants to get in the festival organizing business, and I understand why. Sometimes I think we are crazy when we come up with yet another idea for celebrating. It not only takes a great deal amount of time but a lot of hard-working volunteers to make it successful. We are all so busy in our own worlds with our jobs, kids, school and church activities it is sometimes hard for communities to find enough volunteers who have the time it takes to make a festival or event successful.

This is the perfect time to bring up some of the unsung heroes whom I consider to be the biggest advocates for those who organize festivals and events. I would be remiss, especially with my background, if I didn't give a shout out to the local media in every small town.

As small town media goes, I have done it all. I have been in the radio business, on the editorial board for the local newspaper, and was general manager and news anchor for a cable television station. Did I ever expect to write or produce the next Pulitzer Prize winning piece in small town America? Probably not, but what I found was that being part of the media in a small town, and having a responsibility to help get the information to the public, was as important as any award sitting on a mantle.

I have spent more hours than I could ever count, covering special events, festivals, tourism activities and any other occasion that might draw attention to our community. Our role would start during the planning stages as we would publicize the committee's needs in an effort to stir up volunteers and would end, usually the day after, as we would conduct post-event interviews with those involved. Any time in between, we would always be there.

Unless it is a story with sensationalized and statewide interest, chances are small town news will never make the state's daily newspapers or big city radio and television news stations. We understand that there is an entire state to cover, so we must depend on our local media to tell the story.

I remember in high school that our local newspaper, *The Kentucky Standard*, was published weekly. It would come out every Thursday morning and people would line up outside the newspaper box in front of the newspaper office to get their first look at what happened in Nelson County in the last week. In those days, you would gain celebrity status if you made the front page of the newspaper.

We have become quite dependent on having good local radio and television stations and a credible newspaper. We never go without knowing what's going on because small town media understand the importance of the immediacy of delivering the news, sports, and weather of the day and they share a competitive, yet amicable, spirit. Sharing of "news scoops" is not uncommon and joint breakfasts with community leaders occur often. There is another and probably more important reason that small town residents appreciate our media. We honestly just like seeing our pictures in the paper, watching ourselves on television, or hearing our voices on the radio. Not unlike people in any size town, we get a real kick out of that.

While we have touched only on festivals and events as huge draws for bringing scores of people to a community, sexy small towns have been successful in developing other tourism attractions that entice visitors to their communities.

Most every town, big or small, has a claim to fame, one thing that makes them special. It may be as simple as being known for someone famous who once lived in the area, or maybe your town is in a very scenic area of the state, rich in natural beauty. Kentucky is proud to have one of the best state park systems in the U.S., with fifty-two state parks, all with their own unique attributes and featuring everything from historic places to recreation. Most of these parks are located in or near a small community and are sometimes the economic engine for these often remote areas.

The National Park System, which is one of Congress's greatest creations, is another prime example of major tourism areas that are often located on the outskirts of small towns all across the country. Here are a few of the popular national parks located near smaller communities:

- Grand Teton National Park: Moose and Jackson Hole, Wyoming

- Acadia National Park: Bar Harbor, Maine

- Katmai National Park: King Salmon, Alaska

- Zion National Park: Springdale, Utah

- Abraham Lincoln's Birthplace National Historic Site: Hodgenville, Kentucky

Visitors to these parks spend millions of dollars in these communities and in many cases are the main source of revenue for local businesses.

I have told you about my love affair with small towns, but I haven't told you that running a close second is my love of the National Park System. So you will understand that on my "bucket-list of life" is to visit every National Park in the U.S. with my National Parks Passport in hand.

Historic preservation also plays a key role in the success of many small communities. People love visiting towns with beautifully preserved, older buildings and even better if they have some sort of historical significance. Madison, Indiana (Pop. 12,500) is one of these towns. Located on the Ohio River, the entire town is designated as a National Historic Landmark District and its downtown, with over 2,000 structures, is on the National Historic Register. Madison has been recognized by the National Trust for Historic Preservation as being one of their "Dozen Distinguished Destinations," which has lured many visitors to town and helped contribute to their overall economic success. *Ladies Home Journal* once called Madison "one of the prettiest towns in the Midwest."

Okay, so you may not have a festival or event in your town, or any attractions that would be of interest to anyone out-of-town, and you may not be the "prettiest town in the Midwest." Don't give up yet. There are other ways to bring people to your town. Do you have a library or other public building where you can house your community's ancestral history? Family history brings out the best in people as they search town after town to learn a little bit more about themselves and their ancestors.

Here's a little tidbit I bet you didn't know (and maybe didn't want to) but second to on-line pornography, genealogy research has become one of the most popular uses of the Internet as so many people have a desire to learn more about their family history. Make sure you have a place where out-of-town guests can sit and discover their lineage and learn more about their ancestors who lived in your community. These people will usually stay for days and the trace their roots from your library to your cemeteries. They will eat and sleep in your town. This is a group you can entice by simply making genealogy information available to them. If you do have genealogy information available, make sure it is noted on your city's website or any other public website that people can browse for information about your community.

*B*ottom line, there is nothing more sexy and charming about a small town than its festivals and events, tourist attractions and the history we share with guests. These things bring out the best in us.

If you have the need to entertain out-of-town guests, these special events are the perfect time to do it. You have built-in entertainment and various food options, and you don't have to cook or plan a thing. These are the best kind of dinner parties, or reason for a picnic.

So, here is my suggestion to you: go to your state's official tourism website. Find the link that lists all the festivals and events in your state. Every state has at least one or two of these sites. Print off the list that includes the calendar of events for the next three months and start planning your weekends. If you want to stay a little closer to home, check out your local tourist agency's website, or stop by your local visitor center for a list of all activities coming up.

So many times, you don't even have to go far to find something fun and affordable to do. What better way to have fun than in your own backyard?

I thought it would be fun to make a list of some of the more unusual and popular festivals in small towns all over the country that you may want to find out more about:

- Fellsmere, Florida (Pop. 3,800)—Home of the Fellsmere Frog Festival

- Little Chute, Wisconsin (Pop. 10,500)—Home of the Great Wisconsin Cheese Festival
- Avon, Ohio (Pop. 11,500)—Home of the Avon Heritage Duct Tape Festival
- Chatham, New York (Pop. 4,250)—Home of the "Film Columbia" Film Festival
- Wakarusa, Indiana (Pop. 1,700)—Home of the Wakarusa Maple Syrup Festival
- Lebanon, Kentucky (Pop. 5,931)—Home of the Kentucky Ham Days Festival
- Clute, Texas (Pop. 10,400) Home of the Mosquito Festival
- Arcola, Illinois (Pop. 2,700)—Home of the Broom Corn Festival
- Pikeville, Kentucky (Pop. 6,300)—Home of Hillbilly Days

And the festival that wins the "Yes, you can celebrate anything and have good time" award is:
- Fruita, Colorado (Pop. 6,478)—Home of the Mike the Headless Chicken Festival.

This festival celebrates a chicken named Mike, with an impressive will to live. He survived for eighteen months after having his head cut off in preparation for food processing. (There is not enough room in this chapter to explain this one and anyway, I couldn't decide whether to laugh or cry in honor of Mike. You have got to Google for more about this one.)

SMALL TOWN *Sexy*

is showing off your small town

in a big way.

"From small beginnings, come great things."

—*Proverb*

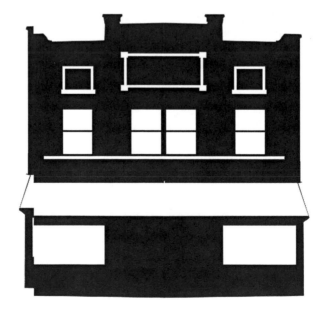

chapter seven

No, Seriously,
Size Doesn't Matter

*S*ince we were very young we have been raised to believe that bigger is always better: "Eat your vegetables so you will grow big."

The bigger the Christmas present, the better the gift.

And the bigger the house you have, the higher level of esteem or wealth.

Now mind you, I would be the first to say that big presents always get my attention first. I can also admit that at some time in my life I aspired to a big fancy house on a spread of land among a lot of old trees.

However, in the perspective of a *Small Town Sexy* lifestyle, I am here to attest to the old adage that "Good things can, and really do, come in small packages."

I made up my own quote one day when I had to justify to some out-of-towners that choosing a life in a small town does not mean you are destined for a life of small things: "The biggest of things happen in the smallest of places."

I have no clue if that is an original quote, or if I heard it somewhere and it stuck with me, but it came to me without any real thought or brain effort. I really think it originated from the heart.

Anybody who knows me knows how much I love living in a small town, and everything that goes with it. They will also tell you that I tend to get a bit defensive with those who criticize my town for whatever silly reason. Don't tell me that my town is not big enough to "make the team" or "make the cut." As we sometimes say here in small towns, "Them there are fightin' words."

You might as well have told me my children are ugly. That's just wrong. If your ultimate loyalty does not lie in small town America, just keep it to yourself.

While attempting to psychoanalyze this defensiveness, I had to turn to my childhood again. From an early age, I can remember being laughed at for being from a small country town.

My dad and Ernest Ruby were coaches for the Bloomfield High School basketball team. For a small town school, we were good—so good in fact that we went to the 1962 Kentucky State High School Basketball Tournament as the Region champs. In the regional championship game, we upset a mighty Taylor County Team, who had Clem Haskins, one of the best players in the state. It was like a scene out of the movie *Hoosiers*, except a last second shot had won the regional finals rather than the state championship. But the excitement was the same, as the fans climbed over chairs and through the bleachers to get to the team on the floor.

In that instance, size did not matter.

For the first time in the history of Bloomfield High School, we were going to the Kentucky State High School Basketball Tournament. We were to be the Cinderella team.

Going to the state tourney is probably the most exciting thing that ever happened to the small town of Bloomfield. Although I was only three and don't really remember it, they tell me that almost everyone in Bloomfield went to Louisville for the game. They say businesses closed and everyone went except for one fireman who stayed in town in case of an emergency, although I am sure that is exaggerated a bit.

As coaches wives, my mother and Coach Ruby's wife, Aunt Edie, were very superstitious. Since our team started winning in the District Tournament they had decided they had to wear the same outfit during each game: red blazers, blue skirts and a white carnation. This was just in case their attire had something to do with the team's winning streak.

Our little Cinderella team fell to defeat in the first game. It was never a real disappointment, considering we were just thrilled to have been able to have such an experience. The fact that such a small school from such a small town had made it to this mighty tournament was a feat in itself. Everyone in the gym, with the exception of our opponents, was cheering for us during that game.

That event brought our community closer than it had ever been before and, perhaps, will ever be again.

My story on how I formed a defensive nature about my town started during my dad's regular season basketball games.

I was around ten years old. We had traveled to a larger town to play a team that we always considered our rival. We had settled in our seats right after the national anthem and fight songs concluded. We were waiting for the tip off when it happened—as loud as thunder on a quiet summer night, it came from the opposite side of the gym:

"Go back, go back, go back to the woods,
Your coach is a farmer and your team ain't no good!"

They repeated it three times and it seemed to get louder with each verse.

Even as a kid those words stung like a wasp and hurt just as much. "The chant from the devil" is how I refer to it today.

My dad is not a farmer, I would think to myself. I do not live in the woods. I live on Main Street across from the post office.

I remember jumping out of my seat and starting down the bleachers heading across that gym floor. My mom came flying down the bleachers after me and grabbed me in mid-stride by my red blazer and put me back in my seat. While I know she didn't like it anymore than I did, her maturity allowed her to ignore it. She said to me in the most serious tone, "Honey, just don't pay attention to them, because that's what they want. They are from the city, and they don't know any better."

I thought to myself, okay, she just wants me to shut up and not get into any trouble. But I was still mad. Sensing that, she leaned over and whispered in my ear, "And anyway, honey, they couldn't find their way out of the city if they had a map and directions." We both just giggled and proceeded to watch the game.

We beat that team by seven points.

I used to wonder if maybe there was something wrong with me. Something buried so deep inside my subconscious that makes my small town desire so strong. I had heard about a phobia where people were afraid to leave their homes or even their city limits. Maybe I had developed a phobia of not wanting to leave small town America—not of physically leaving town, but losing that nostalgic feeling that is so strong to me. If I went somewhere else, would my strong sense of home still be there?

It wasn't until I started writing this book that I found I was not alone in my passion and infatuation with small town life. People would say to me, "Oh, my God, I love small towns too and could never, ever live anywhere else." I was not alone in this small town lover's universe.

I have sat on park benches, by swimming pools, in auditoriums, at bars listening to dozens of small town stories and learning exactly what it is that people find so "sexy" about their own communities. It's like once I started asking, the flood gates opened and the water hasn't calmed since. Men, women, teenagers, and especially my "golden year" friends, all have inspirational small town love stories. A couple of my favorites were posted on my *Small Town Sexy* Blog. To understand and appreciate this deep-rooted feeling, you need to read the following stories:

It seems that the first twenty-one years of my life were perfect. I know that cannot be the case but every memory I have is one of happiness in our family home in Bardstown, Kentucky. This memory issue is probably some version of early senility. None the less, my small town memories are all about "kick the can" very late into the evenings (and trying to keep the bats out of our hair), swimming all day long (until mother was honking the horn from the top of Country Club Hill), bicycling all over the town, sleeping on the porch with the ceiling fan humming on very hot evenings, Cherry Cokes and Nabs at the drugstore after school, hot lazy summer days at the farm and Bourbon Open weekends. All of these memories and many more are surrounded by laughter of family and friends.

I have lived in New York for thirty years—very happily. Much of this adult happiness, I believe, is the result from the security of growing up in my small town. My family and friends gave me the confidence to try everything and not worry about success or failure. Just strive for happiness. They have loved me for all of my craziness—-loved me for who I am. It's as if I have had this dynamic small town supporting me to pursue every opportunity no matter where I go. Life gets extremely busy for everyone these days. But for me, it takes one trip into town and I feel a great sense of comfort and renewal. There is a voice that whispers as soon as I hit the Bardstown line. A voice that gives me great happiness every time I come to town. My heart will always be in small town Bardstown, Kentucky. And the magic that it brings to my life.

—Julie Talbott
New York, New York

What truly makes a small town alluring! It is the people!! Their kindness. Yes they are noisy, yes they can be gossipy, but mostly they are your neighbors. They care and are there in a pinch. We recently went through the power outages due to the windstorm in the fall of '08 and the ice storm STORM of '09, and let me tell you as hard of an experience as it was it was also such an eye opener. People came out of their houses to take care of others. In the fall it wasn't so bad, the weather was nice and we just kind of mingled outside and had cookouts. We visited and enjoyed each other. People would knock on the door to make sure you were okay and just sit and talk. Then the ice storm hit and we all just hunkered down together. The churches had shelters for those who had nowhere else to go and the people provided food for so many. It took several days for the "help" from the government to arrive and we just took care of ourselves. The farmers got their tractors out and moved the debris off the road, the churches provided shelter, neighbors fed each other. If someone had heat they invited others to share it, if someone had WARM water others came to the house to *take a shower. At that moment, I realized I truly wanted to live nowhere else but in my small town!*

—Jeana Berry
Clinton, Kentucky

*S*mall towns, big towns and every size in between all have their social gathering places. I don't mean the bars or the bingo halls, but the places most of the community goes on a regular basis. Mine seems to be the grocery store. After decades of shopping, I have pretty much figured out the best times to go to the grocery. However, on occasion, I will do a reconnaissance drive-by to see just how many cars are in the parking lot, which often turns out to be my determining factor for shopping then or later.

I'm a speed shopper. I have my list, I know the aisles and I try to get in and out. And by the way, beware of Senior Day. Those guys are serious about their ten percent discount, and wait to shop until that one day every month. I say that with all the affection in the world, because my dad is one of those shoppers.

However, as speedy as I try to be, it never seems to work out that way for me. It's not a painful experience because I dislike grocery shopping, but because it tends to be an extended social event in a small town. I honestly think there are people who like the social aspect of grocery shopping and take their time in the aisles in an effort to see and talk to as many people as possible. If you don't see old classmates between the ten-year span of your high school reunions, more than likely you will run into them at your local supermarket at the end of the day—when you are tired and looking your worst, and long to get home.

That is why you will often see me in the store with a ball cap and sunglasses. Remember, I'm here to get in and out. This one shopping day, no ball cap, no sunglasses, and ten full-blown conversations later, I was finally checking out. It took me forty-five minutes to buy seven items. I have to admit that I do know a lot of people and a lot of people know me.

That is a part of living in small town America. However, as a former radio and television news reporter and, for many years, co-anchor of the nightly news on PLG TV-13, people know me. When you are on television in a small town, people feel connected to you and feel comfortable talking with you—even if you are in the aisle trying to decide which toilet paper is the softest.

My only real fear of shopping in my hometown is running into a former principal or high school crush while pulling a box of tampons or anti-wrinkle cream off the shelves. I have been known to buy those late at night.

As an example, let me tell you about ten people I had conversations with during a single small town grocery shopping experience:

- There was the teacher I hadn't seen since my senior year in high school (even though I never saw much of him then either, because as a cheerleader, I was always finding excuses to get out of class to plan for the next pep rally).

- There was the guy I always had a crush on who was two years older than me (age had not been good to him and I was relieved now he never was "that into me.") This could have been my husband!

- In between those conversations, I talked with a neighbor about our ice damage, my daughter's high school friend, who at age nineteen, had just had a baby, my former yard boy looking for some extra work, a lady who used to work with my mom and who always flirted with my dad, my postal lady, and the sushi bar guy who makes the best spicy shrimp roll around.

- There was another lady in her fifties who I did not know, but who pulled a résumé from her purse and ask that I keep her in mind for future employment. After twenty-five years, her husband had just lost his job when a local factory shut down. I gladly accepted it.

- And finally, a friendly and familiar face at the end of the aisle. It was one of my best friends, Alice, whom I had already talked with earlier that afternoon to debrief about the day's events. We talk every day, sometimes twice. Her husband, Dick, is the mayor of Bardstown, so we always act like his "cabinet advisors" and give him our perspective on the "issue of the day." It was great to see her and catch up again as if we had never spoken just hours before.

However, my joy in seeing her was overshadowed by a wave of unworthiness when she showed me a beautiful, beef tenderloin she had bought to cook that weekend for her family, along with fresh asparagus. I thought to myself, maybe if I slowly put my shopping basket behind my back, she wouldn't notice that all I had for my weekend was sushi, soy sauce, a head of lettuce and flavored water. Once we finished talking, I backed all the way out of the aisle, basket behind my back. Afterwards, I took a quick trip back to a couple of departments for a pot roast, potatoes and carrots (something worthy of cooking). My shopping excursion was complete.

I'm really just joking when I complain about the time it takes me to get through the grocery—I don't think I would want it any other way. In small towns, weekly shopping excursions are social activities and it is a great place to catch up with old friends. I don't know what I would do if I landed in a town where no one knew me and I was a stranger in the grocery. Other than getting my shopping completed in only a matter of minutes, I certainly would miss out on this one way we entertain ourselves in small town America.

*Y*ou don't have to live in a big city to have a busy lifestyle. Nationally, we have become a busy society that has mastered the art of multi-tasking. We go to work, fit several meetings in during every day, go home to housework, yard work, homework, and ball games. In addition to those daily tasks, we volunteer at church, help out relatives, and find time for shopping, washing the car, and taking the dog to the vet.

Multi-tasking has become a way of life for most of us. Whether you go into an office every day or work from your home, we all have way too much to do. Many people like this are finally saying "enough is enough" and are chucking their corporate or other overly intense profession. They are opting for something different, something a little more laid back, which allows for more fun and less work.

Small town America is seeing more of these former workaholics who have fled their fast-paced lifestyles and opted for a life without traffic and noise, a life where you can spread out and enjoy open spaces and a life where you can have the option of moving a bit slower.

⬿⬿

While this has been going on for decades, it now has a name. It is called "reinvention." This buzzword will be mentioned many times because small towns, in so many cases, play a critical relocation role with a person who wants to reinvent their life and try something new. It happens every day across America. Someone leaves their big city career and their big city life for what they hope will be something a little less complicated in a smaller town. Size no longer really matters to these people. They have been there, done that. Now it's about a new life in a fresh environment that this time a company hasn't selected for them. They get to choose where they want to live. Many are choosing small towns as their new homes in this reinvention process.

Reinvention doesn't just happen from big city to small town, it is happening in every size community. However, in a small town it is more prominent because these people are newcomers and we are more apt to learn about their stories than someone doing the same thing in a larger city, where anonymity is a way of life.

Being from the same area for most of my life, I think people who make this kind of a dramatic change are adventurous spirits encountering a new journey in life. I really admire those who can just pack their bags and move to a new community, maybe someplace they never knew existed until they started their search. To me it sounds as intimidating as going bear hunting with a pocketknife, and I am not sure I am up for that adventure and potential encounter of the unknown.

Every few months or so, someone will stop by or call me and tell me the story of how they decided, for one reason or another (and believe me the reasons are diverse), to leave an old life behind and start again. On occasion, I have heard some truly bizarre stories and have often wondered if these people were in the witness protection program. Their stories of where they were and why they left are often filled with voids and gaps of information. We don't care what reason brought them to us. We open our small town arms, embrace them and welcome them "home."

Sitting and listening to these stories, I have found that people generally move to areas they have read or heard about, or have family or friends who live nearby.

I love it when a potential "newbie" shows up in my office with a book or a magazine where they have read about Bardstown and its attributes, and it piqued their interest to the point that they wanted to see it.

It's a bit humorous, because I will actually be interviewed, like a parent looking for a nanny, to see if my town can pass their livability test. I love these guys. They are so passionate about their future home and I admire them for taking the initiative to strategically research it right.

National magazines like *Where to Retire, Southern Living* and AAA's *Home and Away Magazine* have been great friends to us, because they have spotlighted our town in a very positive way in their various publications. You know your town has become "someone" and has made the equivalent of "celebrity" when you have an article in one of these popular magazines.

Statewide, we get a lot of coverage in magazines like *Kentucky Living, Kentucky Monthly, Today's Woman* and *The Lane Report*. The chamber of commerce, tourism and economic development offices realize how popular these publications are, especially to small town enthusiasts looking to explore, because our phone calls increase and our website hits spike. It's pretty *Small Town Sexy* when one of these magazines spotlights your town. Not only does it popularize your town statewide, but more importantly, there is a sense of pride among the locals when someone, outside the community, "sings your praises." It's like having your child honored in front of the entire school.

Consider yourself one of the lucky ones in life, if your job or life post-job offers you the chance to live virtually anywhere in the world. If you had that option, where would you choose? A life where the weather is warm and beaches go on for miles? Or maybe you would choose a life in the city, where a maintenance-free condo and a "no vehicle required" world is what you have wanted all your life. It is fun to daydream about picking your ideal location because the amazing options are endless.

In the real world, not everyone has that option. We are usually connected to where we live because of the job we have and family-related obligations.

Or what if it were decided for us at an early age? What if we had no choice in where we wanted to live? And what if our options in our hometowns were so limited that our families decided that to better ourselves, we would have to leave the place we loved and have known all our lives?

That's what happened to Betty Sayers and Nancy Herhahn, two sisters who grew up in rural Nebraska.

These sisters were told by their parents and teachers that they would have to leave rural Nebraska if they were ever going to, as they put it, "make something of themselves." So after school, they did just that.

Nancy eventually ended up in Chicago and San Diego via corporate America, while Betty landed in North Dakota followed by Minnesota with a career in education and writing.

Both had the opportunity to experience an urban lifestyle, but it was not enough. They wanted to come back to their rural roots, to a life that they say, "Mattered—with family connections, meaningful work and a healthy lifestyle." They returned to Nebraska.

Despite the reputation that rural Nebraska had gained in the media as a place with a declining economy and out-migration of rural youth, what these sisters saw were communities with a nurturing quality of life and prosperous entrepreneurial businesses. Once home, they launched a mission to change the negative perception of rural Nebraska by using the skills they learned in the big cities.

That's when the website www.NebraskaRuralLiving.com was born.

Towns like Holdrege, Nebraska, are not only of interest to natives like Betty and Nancy. Newcomers have also learned that life in rural Nebraska is good, with good communities and even more important, good people. One of these newcomers was fortunate to move next door to Betty.

Phil Soriede is not considered a small town guy by birth, since he grew up in Denver, Colorado. The only bit of small town life that he got growing up was visiting his grandparents' farm in South Dakota and working for a veterinarian in a nearby small town. So a move to Holdrege, Nebraska (Pop. 5,600) was going to be a life-changing event.

The question that Soriede heard constantly when he moved to Holdrege was why did he and his wife decide to pack up their family and move to Nebraska? Why not a more exotic state like Texas or Florida? Why not a bigger and more glamorous city?

Soriede says, "My wife was leaving a high-level and high-stress job in a large law firm and saw a job advertised for a library director on the library association's website. While the ad mentioned very little about the position, it described that job would be in a storybook Midwestern town with brick streets and big trees." It was that ad that enticed Soriede and his wife to go and take a look, to see if this town was for real. It was.

The most delightful thing that Soreide says he and his family have found since moving to Holdrege is the wonderful sense of community. "While we lived in neighborhoods and suburbs before, we only kind of knew our neighbors. Here, we have a wonderful group of friends and acquaintances, more than we have had even in the bigger cities. It's nice to go to the park, the grocery store or a high school event, and you know you're not a stranger."

Although an "import" to Holdredge, Soreide has become one of the town's biggest cheerleaders. His paying job is being a one-man ad agency, cleverly named "One Good Ad Guy." He also uses his advertising agency experience as the editor of Betty and Nancy's "Nebraska Rural Living" website and e-newsletter.

After reconfiguring the website to make it more of an e-magazine, they started focusing on the people who are successful and living in rural areas. The new site was launched in January 2006 and started getting about 500 visitors a month. It now boasts over 14,000 visitors every month.

"We want people to know that just because we live in rural America, we aren't hicks from the sticks. There are sophisticated people with various degrees or education as well as political opinions. Small towns are full of successful business people doing very interesting things," Soriede says.

Soriede said he wouldn't be honest if he didn't admit to missing a few of the big city amenities, which on the top of his list is a variety of true ethnic restaurants. On the entertainment side, he says while Holdrege does not have the arts that the big city offered, it does have a state-of-the art performing arts center that seats over 800 people, and hosts a wonderful concert series each year. He believes that small town life is a good lifestyle without many barriers that cannot be overcome.

According to Soriede the sexiest things about small towns are their sense of community, security, affordability, relaxed lifestyle, and the wide-open spaces, where within minutes of anywhere, you are at the edge of town and the sky just opens up.

He admits that he and his wife are a bit more unusual than most of the people they know because they see their life today as their small town chapter. Most of their friends and neighbors have had some small town background. For them, it has been a new and wonderful discovery.

Phil says ten years ago you didn't hear these types of reinvention stories. "Most of us stayed in a town for a lifetime or at least until a career or family commitment forced a change in location. Nowadays I see it happen more frequently." He agrees that our society has become more mobile and that the spirit of finding an exciting lifestyle or maybe even a slower lifestyle has great appeal to many people. "It doesn't matter what size of town you locate to, what's important are the opportunities you make for yourself there."

*T*here are still some mighty vocal naysayers out there that believe if you want to be successful in today's world you have to be in the big city. In small town America, the ideas must be small and the lifestyle even smaller, right? These attitude-copping individuals are the ones I would love to have in a small room for, let's say, about two hours, with about five of my favorite small town activists, and slowly read this book to them two or three times, so maybe, just maybe, we might reprogram their way of thinking. Or even better, give me a day with them in a sexy small town—I have been known to convert a few.

There are many small towns starting to mimic big cities. Many are making gains in technological infrastructure, some are discovering that national retailers are becoming more interested in locating there, and others have become home to new fast food and sit-down restaurants. But the lucky towns, the ones that I lust after on occasion, are the ones that have certain facilities that make them seem larger than they are and make even the largest of cities envious.

Case in point: a small town with a college.

So many colleges in the country today have realized when it comes to delivering a good education, the school and community size does not matter!

I have tried, on occasion, to get Washington County Judge Executive John Settles and my good friend and counterpart Hal Goode of Springfield, Kentucky (pop. 2,863) out of town long enough to try to annex their local college, St. Catharine College, into my county and call it my own. Our counties border each other and the college is only a few miles from my county line. However, knowing I have been threatening this for years, I am sure they have the border patrol prepared to pick me up at the county line at a moment's notice.

In Kentucky, we are blessed with many smaller colleges located in towns with less than 20,000 people. Towns like Springfield with St. Catharine College, Danville with Centre College, Campbellsville with

Campbellsville University, and Georgetown with Georgetown College, just to name a few, are extremely lucky to have these educational institutions in their communities.

The campuses are not large. Most of them have very little student housing. However, the quality of education at these learning institutions is equal to many of their much larger counterparts.

As perception goes, there are still people today who equate the size of the town and college to the quality education you can expect. The bigger the town, the better the college, and thus you are able to offer a superior education.

Don't tell that to the folks at Centre College in Danville, Kentucky whose campus is located in the heart of small town America and is home to over 1,200 students. Centre continues to be ranked as one of the top colleges in the country today, and in 2009, was named one of *U.S. News and World Report*'s "Top 50 National Liberal Arts Colleges in the U.S." To add to its fame, Centre was also the site of the U.S. Vice Presidential Debate in 2006, the smallest college to ever host a national election debate.

Even with their peers, there are some small colleges that don't get much respect. Just ask Dr. David Svaldi, president of Adams State College in the small town of Alamosa, Colorado where the population in 2005 was just over 8,600 people.

Dr. Svaldi became increasingly frustrated when his counterparts, at some of the larger colleges in Colorado, kept teasing him about his "little college." It was this frustration that inspired him to write an op-ed piece for his local newspaper promoting the fact that size really doesn't matter when it comes to education. He appropriately titled his article, "Small colleges in small towns 'rock.'"

As the president of a small, rural four-year college, I find myself required to travel to Denver way too often. Although I enjoy interacting with my colleagues, state legislators, and other officials, I sometimes feel patronized, perhaps because I am from a small town or perhaps because the college I head is tiny.

"How are things in the ice box?" They joke. "You have such a cute little college—how's your enrollment?"

If I have been unlucky enough to have been stuck in traffic on Interstate 25 during my trip, I am tempted to respond: how can you live with wasted hours commuting, road rage, wasting even more time in line at the packed shopping mall, paying $5 for 25 cents worth of coffee? And, really, how often do the traffic challenges of Denver deter you from taking advantage of the many cultural opportunities?

Once, in a conference-call meeting, the group on the other end of the line laughed derisively when they heard the train steam whistle through my office window. Indeed, the city mouse has always felt superior to their country cousin, and often urban folk make fun of the increasingly rare rural lifestyle. How can one live without a shopping mall, Starbucks, Barnes and Noble, a symphony orchestra, and other opportunities for sophisticated, enlightened urban culture?

But many of us find the quality of life in rural Colorado is inversely proportional to the quantity of our population. The crime rate is low in our community: many of us seldom lock our doors, and you can send your kid to the swimming pool by themselves without worry. Our definition of a traffic jam is waiting two minutes on First Street in the middle of our campus. Even people with longer commutes have it relatively smooth: twenty miles in twenty-five minutes between neighboring towns.

In the summer we have free music in the park and easy access to the mountains and wide open spaces. The conclusion of long weekends finds streams of Denverites returning to the city from our idyllic countryside. The relatively low cost of living here attracts a substantial artistic community, and a variety of local bands and Mariachi groups bring joy to all of us. We also enjoy inexpensive performances in intimate venues by groups like the Colorado Symphony Orchestra and David Taylor Dance Theatre.

There are churches in every San Luis Valley community and neighborhood, and our children have a higher percentage of two-parent families than those in urban areas. You can purchase a nice home for less than $150,000 and buy anything you need in our picturesque downtown. You can even get a cup of coffee for less than $5!

Yes, my college of 2,500 students is tiny compared to behemoths like Ohio State and Penn State, or even CSU and CU. But visitors to our *campus from two different accrediting organizations have noted the strong sense of community present on our "tiny" campus. Larger institutions are spending millions of dollars to recreate a sense of a small community within their campuses. On our campus, it's free and genuine.*

I can only echo the sentiment of John Mellencamp's song "Small Town":

> *"No I cannot forget where it is that I come from,*
> *I cannot forget the people who love me.*
> *Yeah, I can be myself here in this small town*
> *And people let me be just what I want to be."*

While Dr. Svaldi admits he never heard anything from his big city counterparts—and that's just fine with him—the article did merit a lot of "Atta boys" from local leaders in the community who agreed they will continue to deal with the "small town image" issue every day. No problem. It won't stop them from continuing to provide a great college experience at one of the best schools in the West.

You have to admit that college towns, big or small, do have a leg up on other communities simply for the fact that they have college students, which means students with money to spend. The majority of these students are not only going to school in these towns, but also living there, which means parents are visiting them, which in turn means even more money being deposited into the local economy. College students today seem set on enjoying college life and appear to have more discretionary income than ever before. Some of the community beneficiaries are bookstores, coffee shops, restaurants, video stores and theaters.

The one very unfortunate fact in all of this is only a very small percentage of small towns will ever become home to a college.

However, that doesn't mean that these other small towns have to do without. That's because God invented the community and technical college system. Well, maybe God did not invent it, but it certainly is a godsend to those hundreds of thousands of students who are able to have an opportunity to attend college and pursue a degree closer to home and at an affordable cost. While community colleges are usually located in a mid-size town, they have arteries of off-campus classrooms in small towns all across the state. This is one way that smaller towns can still offer post-secondary education as well as workforce development opportunities to their residents who are not able—or do not desire—to attend a four-year college.

In Bardstown, we do not have a college or a full-time community and technical college campus, but we receive the off-campus educational benefits of both St. Catharine College and Elizabethtown Community and Technical College. For a small town this is really is "the next best thing to being there."

☙❧

I have visited many of the fortunate small towns that are home to two- or four-year colleges and universities and from the moment you arrive, you can sense the youthfulness and vitality. Colleges bring talented young adults with ideas that add a sense of cool to any community.

There are cool small college towns all across the country. If you were to ask anyone in Ohio what is one of the coolest small college towns in the country, I will bet that the majority will quickly tell you Oberlin, Ohio (Pop. 8,330), home to Oberlin College. The college is a nationally ranked, private liberal arts college and home to the Oberlin Conservatory of Music. The college is located in the downtown area, so every day during the school year, there are 2,000 to 3,000 students in downtown Oberlin, attending classes and hanging out at the local coffee shops, book stores, retail stores and restaurants. Only around ten percent of students bring cars with them, so they tend to walk everywhere.

I first learned about Oberlin College from a friend of mine who is an assistant professor of emerging arts there. Julia Christensen loves Oberlin. She says it is everything you dream about in a small town. It has a park in the town square, quaint businesses line the square, and Oberlin is never lacking for diversity in its cultural offerings like concerts and recitals, art shows and visiting lectures.

Julia should know what she likes in a small town, since she visited many during an extended academic road trip in 2003 and 2004. It wasn't your typical throw-your-bags-in-the-car-and-I'm-taking-off-to-see-the-country kind of trip, rather, it was a project. This project would eventually bring her fame as an author and speaker.

In the winter of 2003, Julia set out to investigate and study the effect that abandoned "big boxes" had on communities and their landscapes. Not the big boxes that you have left over after the installation of a new television or grill, but the massive buildings that companies like Wal-Mart and Kmart abandon when they leave one area and move to a larger, more modern facility.

The idea began in her hometown when she became interested in how Bardstown, Kentucky, was shifting and changing in relation to the county courthouse offices being moved out of the central downtown area. These offices would be relocated to a new and larger Justice Center, on the site of a former Wal-Mart building.

Thus her interest in big box reuse began.

After spending weeks Googling and determining what communities had been creative in their reuse of big box stores, she decided to crisscross the county and find out more. She spent days and nights on the road talking to community's leaders and residents, and documenting these examples herself.

Julia discovered more than she expected on this road trip—she soon knew she was on to something.

A website was launched to publicize her findings and to display photos she had taken along the way, showing how many communities had made lemonade from the lemons of abandoned buildings they had been left with. Instantly, she became an expert on big box reuse. People wanted, and needed, to learn more if they were going to clear their communities of the mess that so often had been left behind. She was asked to speak at city councils and universities, and to display her photos of these examples of big box reuse at various art shows.

Four years after this project began, the book, *Big Box Reuse*, was born. Published by MIT Press, this award-winning book documents ten communities Julia visited that had addressed a big box reuse in their community. Some of the more innovative reuses included churches, schools, courthouses, and—my personal favorite—a museum dedicated to the food product Spam.

Julia says, "One of the main points of the book is to raise awareness among communities and empower them to make these decisions from the ground up, rather than helping the corporation make the decision from the top down. Communities can put regulations in place, like the case in Bardstown, where Wal-Mart was asked to berm their parking lot and put more emphasis on a design that was community appropriate. These things can be done in a small town and we do not have to settle with accepting the homogenous building plans over and over again."

Julia has not always lived in small towns. While she has lived from coast to coast, both in New York City and San Francisco, she still calls herself a small town girl. "I am happy whenever I am involved in a community and occupation I love. There are times where I have clicked in a city and it has worked out, but when it comes down to it, I absolutely feel more comfortable in a smaller vibrant community."

Julia believes there is something to be said about a community based on proximity—people who live next door and on the same street. "Small towns seem so special when you see your neighbor getting a cup of coffee in the morning, see your friends at the post office, and pay your electric bill to a person who knows us by name. It is these small town interactions that give a community the richness and spectrum that is unique."

I asked Julia, since I consider her a community expert, what makes a small town "sexy"? While she quickly said it was the simple, quality of life she experiences every day, the professor in her came out and wrote a list:

1. Not having to commute: Time is valuable to me and a pedestrian lifestyle is awesome. I can get to anywhere I need to be in Oberlin in just a couple of minutes.

2. Knowing the people: Like I said earlier, seeing friends on the street or in the stores or even when you're paying your bills, give you a stronger sense of community and quality of place.

3. Cost of living: I live on the first floor of an old Victorian house.

The amount I pay for rent is one-third what I paid in Manhattan for one tiny room.

4.   Social spontaneity: In large cities I have to plan when and where I am going and give myself plenty of time to get there. Just the other night a friend of mine called me at 10:30 p.m. and invited me over for a quick cup of tea. So I just walked over there and we just caught up about the day. I told him that this would have never happened in San Francisco or New York because it is more difficult to arrange those "spontaneous let's-talk-about-the-day" get togethers.

Does Julia believe that growing up in a small town helped define who she is today? Without hesitation, Julia replies, "Absolutely!"

"I am best friends with Ann Barnes who I have known since I was five years-old. Despite living in different places we still talk on the phone three times a week. It's funny when I tell people who didn't have experiences like that growing up—they are like, 'What, you still talk to people you knew when you were five?'" Julia says she shocks them even further when she tells them that her mom and Ann's mom have known each other since age five, too.

There is a continuity in Julia's life that has also helped define who she is. "I still love to play cards with my grandmother and her friends when I come home. These are eighty-five-year-old women who have known each other all their lives. Having that kind of continuity in relationships in my life is definitely a big part of who I am."

SMALL TOWN *Sexy*

is knowing that size is irrelevant

when creating quality of life and a sense of place.

"Without a sense of caring,

there can be no sense of community."

—Anthony J. D'Angelo

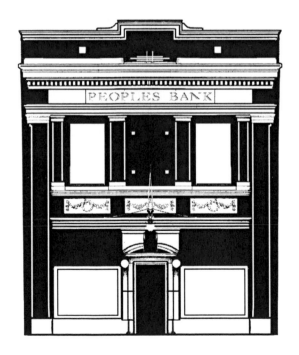

chapter eight

FINDING YOUR
RUBY RED SLIPPERS

I can remember the very first time I watched *The Wizard of Oz*. I was six years old.

I sat just inches away from our black and white television set and never moved. I was totally mesmerized with Dorothy and the lovable characters she encountered on her way to the Emerald City to meet with the wonderful Wizard of Oz.

I went through the whole gamut of emotions watching that movie. I cried when Dorothy had to leave the Scarecrow, Tin Man and Cowardly Lion in the end, and I laughed when the Scarecrow kept constantly falling down and losing his insides. And today, I am still traumatized by those horrifying flying monkeys. I think many kids in my generation never saw monkeys quite the same after that.

But my favorite part of the movie is when Dorothy magically finds herself wearing the ruby red slippers, and she closes her eyes and clicks her heels and says, "There's no place like home, there's no place like home." On the edge of my seat, I had my fingers crossed hoping that those red slippers would take her home, to the place she loved and wanted to be once again.

If it were only that easy! There has been many a day, where I was wearing my own red slippers, (maybe not jewel encrusted) and hoped that by clicking my heels they would take me away, back to the comfort of my house, where my dogs were waiting for me, and the rest of the crazy world would just have to wait another day.

It's not always that easy for everyone who wants to come home. Life has become so much more complicated. We have become so dependent on jobs and a certain type of lifestyle that coming home is not an option. But what if it was? What if after many years of being away the desire is overwhelming and you have to find a way to make it happen?

Some very clever researcher coined the word "boomeranger" to refer to those former residents who return home after leaving their hometowns to go to school or go to work.

The "brain drain" is having a serious effect on the young professional talent shortage in small towns across the country. This phrase is used to define the loss of a community's intellectual labor force to more favorable environments. This group is mostly made up of college graduates who decide to take their education to a city with more to offer.

Once they are gone and get a taste of career choice options and cultural experiences, it is often difficult to lure them back. They have tasted the good life, and it often takes something pretty significant to bring them back.

Small towns cannot compete with offering big city amenities like arts and entertainment and a next-generation nightlife designed for the twenty- and forty-year-olds. What they do have going for them is nostalgia. Good old fashioned, hit 'em with their childhood memories lifestyle—where they remember a better time, a time when they were in a good place, with good friends and family. If they remember a wonderful childhood, they may decide that is what they want for their own children and consider returning home when it's time to have a family.

Small towns need to learn what is attractive to this age group and what they can do to lure them home. To find out what we can do to make this happen, I searched out the best.

There's not a lot that Rebecca Ryan doesn't know about the wants and the needs of the "next generation," a term her company uses for the twenty- to forty-year-old age group.

The founder of Next Generation Consulting of Madison, Wisconsin, Rebecca and her staff are considered the leading experts when it comes to understanding how to engage, attract, or even just retain, the next generation age group. Next Generation works with companies and communities all across the country in determining ways to make them better places for the next generation of talent. As well as running a company and being a national speaker, Rebecca was inspired to write the book, *Live First, Work Second,* which enlightens readers to the fact that this age group is placing more emphasis on where they live than where they work.

Rebecca will admit that her experience is biased in the fact that most of the communities she works with are those with populations of 100,000 or more. However, she has seen a trend and says if her hunch is correct, that there will come a point at which time we all eventually become nostalgic for home no matter what size community we are from.

"I think really smart communities, big or small, are grabbing on to this boomerang concept and are looking at it as a perfect target market These folks do not need convincing about what their hometown is and isn't. It is comfortable and familiar to them, which could be their first step in coming home," Rebecca explained to me.

Rebecca adds, "You know it's true that people move more for feeling than for fact. For example, no one would be driving a Hummer today if people made purchases only based on factual information. You have to appeal to the hearts and the heads of these people, and nostalgia is a big, big motivator. And nostalgia is all about home."

Smart communities are doing a lot of innovative things to lure this twenty- to forty-year-old age group back home. Leaders are recognizing that so many of these former residents, now young professionals, come home for the holidays to visit family and usually have three or four days before having to go back to their real lives. In many instances, during these holidays, communities are welcoming them back and reintroducing them to their hometown—showing how things have progressed, like the addition of new or renovated retail centers, unique restaurants and coffee shops and new living opportunities.

Ryan tells the story about a bank in a small town in Nebraska that offers bus tours of their community to former graduates when they are home for the holidays. While it's not your typical high school homecoming event, it does get former students together talking about their hometown and the positive things that have happened since they have been gone from home.

So what does Rebecca think is *Small Town Sexy* for the next gen group? She reflects on her company's client in Lake Jackson, Texas. The employees they have helped recruit all have one thing in common—the love of the outdoors.

"They love knowing that they can buy a fair slice of the outdoors for a lot less money than Houston, Texas, would have allowed them." She also added that a quaint atmosphere is important, especially to those with young children because of their requirements for good schools and safe streets.

And then, for those hyper-achiever types, Rebecca says the concept of being a big fish in a small pond is very attractive and sexy. "They like to be where they get asked for their input and where they are able to make an impact on where they live. And, that is very important."

Small towns are going to have to make opportunities available if they want to entice this generation back to their towns. Rebecca's group is able to survey an area and find out firsthand what it will take for the expatriates to return home. Many larger communities are taking their "show on the road"—visiting other cities, hosting events and inviting former residents out for the evening. Their goal is to describe to this group all the new opportunities that await them, should they choose to move back home. I have always thought this was an exceptional idea and one that apparently does work.

I can't think of anything more *Small Town Sexy* than being brought up in a town you love, go away and have a stimulating career in a big city, and return home to family and a job that you have dreamt about for years.

Welcome to the world of Dawn Ballard Przystal. A true boomeranger if there ever was one.

If you had asked anyone in Dawn's family, or her friends ten years ago, if they thought she would be home living in the same town where she grew up, the answer would have been a quick no. Although born and raised in a small town, a product of parents who were both reared in even smaller towns, Dawn was always a bit different. Though a small town girl from her roots, she always had a big city nature about her and could see things outside her small town box.

After graduating from Western Kentucky University, Dawn followed her father's profession in the newspaper business, not on the editorial side, but in a variety of other departments. Her last department switch landed her in advertising sales for a newly-developed Let's Tour America group travel publication. This job took her all over the South and East visiting some of the best tourism destinations in the country. After a year, Dawn knew it was time to move on and take her career to a bigger city with more experiences and opportunities.

Dawn says, "I really wasn't sure where I wanted to go, but I knew it had to be a big city with good airport accessibility. It was 1996 and Atlanta was busy with the Summer Olympics, so I knew it was too crazy to go there. Chicago, well, it was just too damn cold. With both of those out of the picture, I knew it had to be Dallas."

Dawn did exactly what Rebecca Ryan said so many next geners do, she moved to Dallas with no job. It really wasn't as random as that—she did have cousins who lived in a suburb of Dallas, so that helped to narrow her decision. Dawn stayed with her family while she became familiar with the city and landed a job.

For eight years, she was a Texan. She worked at various businesses, including a bank, tourist attractions, and an international customs company. It was pretty exciting for a girl in her twenties from small town America. Life was good.

You can imagine my surprise when I got a phone call from Dawn telling me she was coming home to attend an award ceremony for her dad . . . and she wanted to stop by and talk to me about her future—a future that she saw in Bardstown.

Bardstown? Did she say Bardstown or did we just have a bad connection? This big city girl, who had been enjoying a wonderful cosmopolitan life in Dallas, wanted to come home to Bardstown? Were her parents ill? Was she? Was she running from a bad relationship? All these crazy ideas went through my mind because so many of her small town friends had been very envious of her life in Dallas; not one would ever think Dawn would want to pack it up and move back home.

Fortunately, none of my speculations about why Dawn wanted to return were true. It was much simpler than all that: it was just time for her to come home.

When she first moved to Dallas and came back home for holidays or other reasons, she would say to herself, "God, I can't wait to get back to the city." However, after being in Dallas for a while, she found herself constantly checking special airline deals so she could fly home more regularly. Every time Dawn got a good deal, she would book it, and spend a few days back in the only place where she really felt at home. As time went by, there didn't have to be a good airfare.

Then one weekend she came home and everything changed. The excitement of going back to Dallas was gone. This time it was incredibly hard to get on the plane and leave "home" behind. Her mind was made up.

But, this time—being a little smarter and wiser—she was adamant: she was not moving anywhere without a job first.

Dawn had expected to go to Louisville, Cincinnati, or maybe Nashville, some larger city, to be able to get another job that really excited her. However, patience paid off, and in less than a year, she was hired when a vacancy developed in the Bardstown-Nelson County Tourism office. Dawn was about to become the vice president of Tourism, Marketing and Sales in her hometown, a job she had dreamed of for years.

I had to ask what enticed her back home to small town America. "I've done it. I followed my dream to the big city. I was young and in my twenties and had a great life in the city, with a great apartment, a doorman and a roof-top pool. And of course it was Dallas, a town that was alive 24/7. Some may think I'm crazy to give up a life like that, but I can honestly say that I followed my heart back home."

Don't think that the "big city" girl in Dawn is gone. She admits a tendency to gravitate to people who have lived outside the "Bardstown bubble," and have some sort of big city life experiences.

She still loves to make her roads trips to Chicago, Cincinnati, Miami, and, yes, back to Dallas to get what she calls her "big city fix." Dawn will admit to you that she misses her options of places to eat, kinds of food and terrific options on airplane flights since you can get from Dallas to just about anywhere in the U.S. on a direct flight.

Bardstown has benefited from Dawn's big city adventures and she has been able to incorporate much of what she learned into her job in tourism. This new knowledge is critical for the innovative growth of any community. Too many small towns get caught up in the "that's not how we do it here" mentality. To survive we must welcome this age group back with open arms and, more importantly, open minds.

I can remember the night of my high school graduation. We had just finished the commencement ceremonies and we were all in the school cafeteria taking pictures with our friends and families. Most of us crying, knowing that chances were, we would all split up and eventually go our own way. What I also remember about that night were classmates who were adamant that they couldn't wait to get away from this place and never come back.

It was a typical emotion for eighteen-year-olds who had spent their entire lives in one place, a place that now seemed to be further from their minds than anyplace else. They couldn't wait to leave.

It's probably hard to believe at this point in the book, but at that moment, I was one of them.

I was very anxious the first day I arrived at the University of

Kentucky for my freshman year. I had been in the same town, in the same environment, and around a familiar group of people all my life. Now I was moving away to live with people I did not know. For the first time, I would be sleeping in the same room with a stranger. I hadn't done that since Junior High School Conservation Camp and I hated it then. I was terrified.

For some reason I had it in my mind that everyone at UK would be from a larger town and I would be the new kid from the small town that everyone would make fun of. I couldn't have been more wrong.

My first night there, I discovered that many of my dorm mates were from towns all around the state, many much smaller than mine. Even though I have great praise for my high school geography teachers, some of my new friends were from counties that I did not even know existed in Kentucky. I also discovered that they, too, had come to school with the same small town anxiety.

To many, Lexington was the largest city they had ever been in and they were in awe of the city's tall buildings and massive structures. We actually discovered that our dorm had more residents than some of our small towns. My fear of being made fun of and not fitting in quickly faded.

I remember many tearful nights when we would be homesick for our families. Then we discovered that the best medicine was to sit around and talk about our hometowns and entertain each other with stories about where we grew up. We talked about our schools, sports teams, the festivals we had, the county fairs, and of course, important things like boyfriends and dating. The majority of the time was spent talking about friends we left behind and we would speculate about what they were doing back home at that moment. It wasn't until then that I realized how much I had taken for granted all those years, and that I was truly blessed growing up in my town. My town is where I had the chance to be a part of so many activities and have a huge extended family of friends just around the corner.

I not only gained new small town friends, but many new big city friends from cities including Louisville, Cincinnati and Nashville. On occasion, we would leave for a weekend and go home with the big city girls and experience the life they had—the abundance of entertainment, shopping and so many opportunities right out their back door. I was in awe that, in just a matter of minutes, they could be at the mall or the movie theatre. Living a life where activities like that had to be planned for days in advance, I was very jealous.

It did come as a surprise to me when my big city friends were anxious to see where we were from and to experience a little of the small town life. We soon discovered they were enchanted by our hometowns and seemed to use the word "cute" quite often. One friend said she expected Aunt Bee to greet her at the door with a plate of cookies.

College graduation is one of those times you find yourself searching for direction in life, wondering about your next step, and where it will lead you. Maybe your desire to live in a small town started with a friend you went home with in college. Maybe your small town roots never left you and the desire to move back came after you had a chance to spread your wings and live in other places.

There is an entirely different group of people, also looking for direction, not at the start of their careers, but, at the end. These fortunate souls, who we all aspire to be like one day, are beginning the next chapter in their lives, and are entering the wonderful world of retirement.

If you haven't already thought about it, then I am sorry to have to break it to you this way: Hey, you're getting older. But, I am a true believer that life really does get better with age.

If you want it to sound a bit sexier, let me put it this way: Are you one of the millions of people who are getting closer to the age when you don't have to wake up to an alarm clock anymore, or sit through hours of unnecessary meetings, and spend your days on the road selling a product? If so, then consider yourself one of the luckiest people in the world, because you must be nearing retirement.

Now that is sexy!

See, that getting older thing doesn't sound so bad now right. Now, you can do what you want, when you want and more importantly you can do it where you want. And it gives me great pleasure to announce that many retirees are deciding that they want to spend the next chapter of their lives in small town America.

A small town you say? What about the days of retirees moving to Florida and Arizona, the land of sun and warmer weather? Fortunately for those states, they continue to see their share of retirees, but there is a different trend that has emerged recently, that includes these baby boomers who are opting for something different, something less conventional.

Small towns have become quite popular with baby boomers as they decide where to spend their retirement years. The opportunity to get away from the fast-paced world, full of crowds and noise, and slow down in a small town, with wide-open spaces is very appealing.

This generation of retirees has worked most of their lives and no longer have career or child obligations, are free of debt, and have a longing for something new. Generally, many of these new retirees will chose towns with warmer climates, with retirement communities, and with good highways or airports nearby. They want and need easy accessibility so family or friends can visit them, or so they can take off at a minute's notice. And because they have remained so active all their life, a large majority of this group is looking for a place where they can have a healthy and energetic lifestyle.

In many cases, these retirees are also looking for areas with recreational offerings like fishing and golf courses. Good healthcare facilities, grocery stores and restaurants close enough to walk to are imperative, and cultural resources are a must. Just because they are retired doesn't mean they plan to slow down. They still have a need to learn new things and to keep up with the trends of the day. Towns that offer continuing education opportunities and cultural opportunities through arts and music will have a better chance of luring retirees to their communities.

Who said you can't come home? That speaks of another type of retiree, the ones that come back to their hometowns after retirement. This is happening more and more as the baby boomers begin thinking about their retirement options. Many of them were forced out of their small communities decades ago because opportunities were limited. Now, they have lived their lives and worked their jobs and feel it's time to follow their hearts—to reacquaint themselves with a community where they have fond memories.

It is a place just like this where the new chapter of Len Spalding's life begins.

Although officially retired as president and CEO of Chase Global Mutual Funds in New York City (now J.P. Morgan Chase Mutual Funds) Spalding apparently didn't get the memo. He continues to be as busy today in his hometown of Springfield, Kentucky, as he was twenty years ago. However the lives of him and his wife, Susan, are now is filled with picking their own projects and diversifying their time with many different activities.

After an initial year in college, a stint in the Army, more college and then on to graduate school, Spalding found his way into the field of finance, which took him away from his Kentucky home for more than forty years. These years were exciting ones, living a life in Chicago and New York in the world of high stakes corporate finance that most people only read about. However, after decades of global traveling, which included some frightening flying adventures, and what he says as "riding that same horse out of the gate every day," he needed something new. This former college basketball player was still in good health and had lots of energy and wanted to go somewhere he could make a difference. Enter small town America, Springfield, Kentucky.

Now instead of one massive project, Spalding divides his time between many civic and philanthropic projects that have meaning to him. Those include serving on the Board of Trustees for Bellarmine University in Louisville and St. Catharine College in Springfield and on the Board of Directors for the Springfield-Washington County Economic Development Authority and the Marion/Washington County Airport. He also is a founder and board member of Glenview Trust Company in Louisville. He has also broadened his scope of ventures, entering the food service business as owner of a multi-store franchise of Snappy Tomato Pizza restaurants.

Even with all this to keep him busy, Spalding continues to serve on the Board of J.P. Morgan Mutual Funds and is chairman of its Investment Policy Committee. He is an example that given good Internet access and an airport nearby, you don't have to give up a big city career after moving to a small town.

Spalding talks about two things that are appealing to him about living in a small town. "In the city, I only knew people in one dimension. Those I knew from work, I never really knew them outside the environment of our jobs. Those I socialized with, I didn't know much about their careers. I never really got to know people in all facets of their life. However, in a small town, you cross paths more often with people and you get to know them in all their dimensions including their work environment, home life, and what they like to do on weekend." Spalding says it even goes further into their ancestry as far as knowing their mothers or grandparents. He adds, "This makes for a very interesting multi-dimensional way of life. And that to me is appealing."

Being the astute business mind that he is, he has another reason why he enjoys life in a small town. "We are actually able to make decisions on the spot and it doesn't have to go up sixteen layers. I have been known to debate issues for weeks and never get anything accomplished. My experiences here are that we make decisions from a full report of information and not just an executive summary and people seem enthused about getting a task accomplished without delay."

Spalding exudes knowledge and confidence when you talk to him and he can sit and debate any issue as if he has just been briefed by a team of experts, so it was a bit unusual when his confidence to move to Springfield was not one hundred percent. "I was scared to death when I got here and remember telling my wife that this may be the dumbest damn thing I have ever done in my life. What was I going to do all day? The last thing I wanted to do was to be bored and be stuck doing the same thing all the time and I was way too lazy to be a farmer."

While childhood nostalgia brings many people home, Spalding was adamant to say that was not his reason. He came back for a sense of obligation, coming back to where he could make a contribution. Spalding gives his wife, Susan, the credit for suggesting they return to Springfield. Now being back, he said he has developed that "sense of community" and that special feeling you get when you know this is home. He says he is thoroughly delighted in the decision he and his wife made.

Spalding recommends this kind of change to anyone who might be leaning in the direction of moving to a small town. "Go for it," he says and not because you are going to have some big payoff but simply because that is how you are going to be happy.

Just ask him to talk about his hometown and any of these projects he has become involved with since returning home. The passion in his voice is evident. He loves this new life in small town America.

In my opinion, the best aspect of these retirees moving into my area or into other small and rural communities is the fact that we now have new faces with new talents that can breathe new life into our communities. These retirees have chosen to spend their life here and they want it to the best it can be.

If you want to get attention from the retirement community, get listed in a national publication that they read. In 2006, Bardstown was listed in *Where to Retire Magazine* as one of "Eight Great Places to Retire with a Top Ranked Hospital." You wouldn't believe the number of relocation inquires we received after that article was published. I find it amazing the number of newly retired people I run into here each year. They are constantly on the go and you will see them at the coffee shop having breakfast, exploring the new releases at the library, taking a walk through downtown, or enjoying a little fun at one of the many events we host. They also have something most of us don't have and that is time. Retirees are some of a small town's best volunteers.

I am one of those aggressively hospitable people—if I don't know someone I will walk right up to them, stretch out my hand, introduce myself, and try to find as much information about how they found their way to Bardstown as I can. It's the years of reporter in me, I guess. My friends ask me why don't I just take them to a darkened room and shine a bright light on them, since it seems as if I am interrogating them. Of course, they are exaggerating a bit. But I always learn something interesting. People love talking about themselves and appreciate when someone wants to hear their story. I don't think I have frightened anyone away yet.

SMALL TOWN *Sexy*

is being an attractive and desirable community

to anyone at any stage in life.

"It's passionately interesting for me that things that I learned

in a small town, in a very modest home,

are just the things that I believe won the election."

— *Margaret Thatcher*

chapter nine

CONFESSIONS OF A
SMALL TOWN POLITICIAN

*I*f you were to believe the television shows of yesteryear, you would have to assume that small town mayors and council people are all a bunch of bungling numbskulls that don't know their way around a town hall.

Some of my favorite moments on television came during the popular series *Newhart*, when the entire community was the town council and decisions were made by a simple show of hands and saying "aye or nay." This was self-governance at its best, democracy, quick and easy, and agreeable.

I am sure there are small communities that continue to follow this majority rule vote taking in the decision making process, but most towns have progressed much further because the issues have become more sophisticated.

Small towns or big cities, it doesn't matter. All communities and towns deserve good governance. Governing that needs to be educated and insightful and protects the public, not only for safety concerns, but in ways concerning the focus for their future.

Even as early as twenty years ago, the most controversial issues in small and rural communities surrounded taxes and road money. Unfortunately, the tax issues have not gone away and probably never will, as long as the public continues to gets taxed on everything from the property they own to their occupations. However, it is road money, and who gets it, that always commands the most attention and stirs everyone up. Those with the most influence that year get the roads paved in their district. It's called patronage. It is what built small town politics. Even today many small towns' decisions get clouded by personal relationships.

What has changed in small town politics? Small towns are getting smarter and care more about the people who are running their communities. It's not about getting your best buddy elected, who, on a bet, wanted to see if he could win a council position. It's now about making sure that leaders are the best qualified and not only have good common sense but strong leadership skills.

I would challenge you to find anyone more knowledgeable about politics in Kentucky than Al Cross.

A former political writer for Kentucky's largest newspaper, *The Courier-Journal*, Al has seen it all. From the big time politics in the state capital, to the small town politics in the various rural communities he has lived and worked in. There is probably not an issue he hasn't written about. He comes by his knowledge of politics naturally as his father, Perry Cross, was a politically active businessman who served as a state representative in the 1940s.

Today, Al is on a different stage, working to raise awareness of the issues in rural America. Now the director of the Institute for Rural Journalism and Community Issues, Cross says, "Small town America has developed a little more of a higher profile in the last year or so due to the number of organizations out there designed to bring awareness to the issues of rural and small town America."

Cross knows national politics as well. When he says that Barack Obama is the most urban president we have had since Franklin Roosevelt, or maybe longer, there is no need to Google that for accuracy. However, with that said, Al goes on to admit that Obama had a rural page on his campaign website and still does today on his White House website, so he is trying to be tuned-in with small towns and rural America.

Small town politics is often about personalities and patronage, but sometimes issues do prevail. Sometimes it is harder to get away from the personality side of politics because of whom you go to church with, whom your son plays in little league with and whom you bank with.

Cross says, "The most successful small town politicians, as far as rendering good public service, are the ones who know how to gain support for an issue before it is even an issue."

He goes on to say that small towns have a lot more honesty about them than larger places. "Because people live closer together they must be more honest with each other and they can't be in the business of putting up a front. It is that authenticity that people still hunger for and that makes small rural communities so alluring," he says.

*R*ural America, especially in the areas of what has been termed Appalachia, has seen its share of economic hardships. An isolated area due to geography, this region continues to be portrayed as a culturally backwards way of life. While there are some truly impoverished areas in Appalachia, there also some small communities that continue to grow and prosper and where their residents would never think of living anywhere else.

Hazard, Kentucky, is one of these towns. No, not the fictional county of Hazzard from the television series *Dukes of Hazzard*, although it does have its share of characters, including my favorite one—who just happens to be the mayor.

For more than thirty years, the small eastern Kentucky town of Hazard, Kentucky (Pop. 5,200), has been led by Mayor Bill Gorman, a man who many believe will be mayor as longs as he wants. At eighty-three years old, Mayor Gorman won his last election with eighty-three percent of the vote, a feat he is very proud to tell anyone about.

According to Mayor Gorman, it wasn't his idea to run for mayor the first time his name showed up on the ballot. He said, "I was single and having the time of my life running up and down the beaches of Florida and a bunch of idiots filed papers for me to run for mayor. I actually won and have been here ever since." Thank goodness for crazy friends. He jokes that people keep electing him because he works for cheap. He does not take a salary and doesn't even like to park in city parking lots.

Hazard is located in the Appalachian area of Kentucky where coal mines have ruled for years. "We are supposed to have around 5,000 people here, but the Census Bureau never gets anything right here in Appalachia. After working with those census workers we came up with a total of 38,000 in Perry County."

There is a lot of pride about living in a small town, and that pride is ever so apparent when it comes to state and federal dollars. Mayor Gorman was contacted by the feds in Washington, D.C., and was asked what he needed in the way of stimulus money—he declined their offer. "I told them we had a balanced budget of $25 million and didn't have any needs, and they should share the money with those towns that are in worse shape than us." He offered that government money comes by incurring some debt and interest and he saw no need for that.

Just ask anyone in Hazard what makes Mayor Gorman such a good mayor and they will tell you it's because he had no background in politics. He was a successful businessman, and runs the city that way. Like so many mayors in small towns, he was not born into politics, but had been in another type of work before entering the world of government. And still today, most small towns only have part-time mayors who work full-time jobs and run the city on their off time.

Prior to his political career, Mayor Gorman had experience in banking, insurance, coal and broadcasting. One of his proudest accomplishments outside of city business happened in the 1960s when he built the first-ever commercial television station in the U.S., which opened his opportunities to meet and interview a lot of national figures. If you ever have some time, let Mayor Gorman tell you about some of his experiences. He can entertain you for hours.

My favorite story involves Pres. Ronald Reagan. Mayor Gorman had an appointment to meet with President Reagan the day he got shot. One of Gorman's prized possessions, hanging in his city hall office, is a letter signed by the president apologizing for not being able to meet with him the day he got shot. Mayor Gorman laughs about the letter. "It reads that he was sorry he couldn't meet with me that day because he had 'problems of his own' to deal with." Of course he was referring to the shooting incident. "I wouldn't take anything for that letter today."

For a businessman and mayor of such a small town, he is rather large in the political arena. He has known every president since Eisenhower, except the second George Bush and Jimmy Carter and according to Mayor Gorman, "I didn't like Carter."

He has yet to meet President Obama; however, I have no doubt that in time, he will be dining with the Obamas.

I had to ask him what he thinks about the comparison made between the fictional town of Hazzard in the *Dukes of Hazzard* television show and his community."

"We capitalize on it," he said. "Anyone who is a VIP and comes to Hazard, or anyone we want to denote as special to our community, is honored with the distinction of being a 'Duke of Hazard'—a sort of key-to-the-city honor." Some notable Dukes include most presidents dating back to Ronald Reagan. Let's not forget the most famous, the Pope. He didn't tell which Pope, but any one of them is pretty impressive. The mayor says, "We get a kick out of it and people seem to enjoy it. It's great publicity for our town."

What is the key to the town and the Mayor's success? Mayor Gorman sums it up in three words, "It's the people. I tell people all over the country that I live in the greatest town in America, that despite some of the issues we are dealt, we are able to survive and grow as a community."

Mayor Gorman also suggests that to have a successful career in politics you have to learn the art of communication. His background in this has served him well. "In small town politics you have to keep people informed every step of the way if you want to get anything accomplished." In his thirty or so years as mayor he has seen no more than fifteen negative votes on his council. He attributes that to talking a problem out and finding a common ground that is agreeable to the entire city commission.

"There are not a lot of classes you take for this," he says. "You live it and learn from it and determine what is the best for the people in your town and for the town's future growth. The decisions are not always popular ones, but are the ones I think best for the city at that particular time."

Mayor Gorman says if he has any one good piece of advice for his fellow governmental leaders in small town America it's this: "Keep one hand on *The Wall Street Journal* and the other on the city. You can learn a lot from both and be successful at it."

Will Mayor Gorman continue another term and is there anyone in Hazard crazy enough to want to fill his big shoes? Mayor Gorman replies, "Ah, these shoes aren't that big. I only wear a 7 ½."

The *Small Town Sexy* in small town politics is that people have a buy in and feel ownership in what they do. You can be involved and make a difference in the community you have chosen to call home. Not only is a decision they make about a water or sewer issue going to affect current residents, but also those for generations to come. They make decisions that are tangible, that you can see and touch, from fixing potholes to building parks and community centers. So very often, there are generations of families who have been making decisions over the years passing the gavel down. This involves a continuity of leadership that has been proven successful to small towns everywhere.

In Bardstown, we are fortunate to have good political leadership that has taken generations to mold and perfect. Bardstown Mayor Dick Heaton is a product of a family that has been in politics since 1935 when his grandfather, Jim Conway, became mayor of Bardstown and served in that office for nine years. In 1966, Mayor Heaton's uncle, and political mentor, Gus Wilson, was elected mayor and served in that role for over twenty years. While being mayor of a small community is a sometimes difficult and often time-consuming position to hold, Mayor Heaton certainly comes by it naturally. Since the age of seventeen, he has been involved in some sort of political campaign, whether behind the scenes in organization or as a political fund-raiser for state and national campaigns.

Mayor Heaton told me, "I was raised with the understanding that involvement in the community is something that is expected of you. Since my grandparents first came here in 1919, my family has played some role in community and civic endeavors."

Most small town mayors are part-time and have "real" jobs and careers they have to focus on. It takes multi-tasking skills to another level and patience beyond belief for their family members.

To be a successful small town mayor, Mayor Heaton says there are two priorities: You must be accessible to the public and willing to listen.

"Running a town is no different from running a business. Regardless of the size of the issue, people want to talk to the top person when they have a problem. I try to be as accessible as possible to handle these issues on a personal basis. In a town our size, we deal with those of all ages and income levels, from the destitute to the affluent. Each person is as important as the other, and deserves to be listened to."

Will the generation of politics continue with Mayor Heaton's sons? "I feel confident that both my sons will remain in Bardstown. While they both are pretty independent thinkers, there is a chance that the generations of politicians will continue with them. Like me, they have grown up in this arena and both would be assets to our community or to our state in future years."

Not everyone is cut out for small town politics. It takes a special person with the right attitude, savvy, time, and most importantly, thick skin to "do a city good." Talk about skeletons in your closet—most people in small towns want to keep their private life just that, private. Sometimes this makes it difficult in small towns to find enough well-qualified people who want to run for any of the many elected positions.

Mayor Gorman admitted early on that he wasn't raised in politics, but was a businessman turned politician. Mayor Heaton says he has been involved in politics since his teenage years. There does not seem to be a cookie-cutter for politicians. It comes to everyone in a different way.

Take Jody Lassiter, for example. Now the president of the Danville-Boyle County Kentucky Economic Development Authority, Lassiter says he must have come by politics naturally since his mother said as a young child he watched the 1976 presidential conventions from start to finish and that he has been a "bit odd like that" ever since. Not odd in the fact that he is peculiar, but odd in the intense passion that he developed for the political process at such an early age.

Lassiter was raised in the town of Almo in western Kentucky's Calloway County, a small town outside the area's largest community of Murray. The town, which was a railroad boom town in the 1890s, was actually named Alamo, until someone misspelled the name and left out an "a." It's been known as Almo ever since.

When he was in high school, Lassiter worked on two statewide political campaigns. It wasn't an easy entry into politics that year since both the candidates he admired and worked so hard for were defeated in their respective campaigns.

While politics was his love, Lassiter knew that he really wanted a career as an attorney and went on to law school after graduation. With a law degree in hand, he returned to Calloway County and right back into politics when he chaired Lt. Gov. Paul Patton's county campaign in his run for governor of Kentucky. They wanted a "fresh face with no scars" and that was Lassiter. The campaign was successful and Patton became the 59th Governor of the State of Kentucky in 1995.

At age twenty-six, he followed Governor Patton to the State Capital in Frankfort, where he first worked in the governor's office and later, as the director of the Department of Local Government (DLG). His job at DLG was what he calls "his cutting of teeth in politics."

"Those years were probably the most rewarding years of my career," he says. "Yes, we had fun handing out the big checks signed by the governor, but the greatest value I received was going to the smallest of towns and counties in the state and meeting the people. Seeing these communities and getting to know their elected officials, many of whom were true characters, were the greatest experiences I had in state government."

There seems to be a consensus about differences in small town and big city politics. Small town politics are personal. The decisions you make, and the stands you take, have a personal effect on someone and in many cases, it may be a neighbor, a friend or even a family member. Someone may win and someone may lose and most will remember who was responsible for making that happen. Local politics are the heart of a community.

Lassiter is adamant in his belief that politics in small towns has changed over the past couple of decades. Magistrates, or county commissioners, as we call members of our county government, have always considered themselves road commissioners. Thirty years ago what mattered to them, in most cases, was the road money or black top money. They occasionally had to deal with tax issues.

He says, "Today, small town politics has evolved into dealing with a variety of issues that may be a microcosm of what is dealt with in Washington, D.C., like emergency services, social welfare, economic development, and other issues within their communities with greater levels of responsibilities. We are also seeing more educated and diverse individuals who are running for and being elected into office. These men and women are looking beyond the boundaries of their own districts. Fiscal Court has become like running a corporate enterprise with the same daily issues and budgetary matters."

"There is no doubt that there is one thing about politics we can all agree on," says Lassiter. "In the South, politics is certainly a contact sport. It can rise to the level of state religion just like bourbon, basketball and horses."

James H. Mulligan, a great Kentucky lawyer and poet, said it best in the last line of a poem he wrote in 1902:

"*. . . the birds are the sweetest in Kentucky,*
thoroughbreds are fleetest in Kentucky,
the landscape the grandest in Kentucky and politics,
the damndest in Kentucky."

There is nothing more fun than a good old campaign and election in a small town. I am sure most will debate whether it brings out the best or the worst in people, but it does tend to be an exciting time.

We don't do polls and don't have a number of analysts dissecting the candidates and their political views. And usually—and I must reiterate, usually—we don't try to go looking for a truck load worth of baggage that a candidate may have and post it on YouTube.

Small town elections are basically pretty harmless. Here is a typical list of things you can expect to see and experience during a small town campaign:

1. Yard signs (I think that candidates truly believe that the number of votes you get are based on the number of signs you put up and whose yards those signs are placed in.)

2. Newspaper, radio and television advertising

3. Flyers stuffed in mailboxes (yes, this is illegal)

4. A good old-fashioned debate or two (In my town these are always very amicable, with the candidates promoting themselves and not the faults of their opponents.)

5. More signs ('nuff said)

6. Door-to-door campaigning

7. Attending every public event two months before the election

8. More signs added during the last week because your opponent did

9. The campaign concludes with a big election night party, celebrating not only a win, but also the fact that the election process is over.

If you want my vote, you need to come see me. Stop by my house, introduce yourself and tell me why I should vote for you. I don't care that you have one hundred signs posted all across the county. That may actually be a vote against you. I cannot find one thing *Small Town Sexy* about cluttering our countryside with political signs.

What is *Small Town Sexy* in small town politics? It's the city council members, fiscal court members, school board members, state representatives, senators, and all the other elected officials who take time away from their families to make decisions about our communities that affect us and the quality of our lifestyle. These elected officials do this for very little compensation and even less appreciation.

SMALL TOWN *Sexy*

is being able to have the opportunity to get involved in the decision making process of your community, county and state.

"I read about eight newspapers in a day.
When I'm in a town with only one newspaper,
I read it eight times."
—Will Rogers

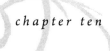

chapter ten

BIG CITY ENVY

*L*et me be very candid with you. I love, love, love Big Cities!
Does that seem to be a contradiction, since the whole point
of this book is to tell you about my love affair with small towns? Is this like
being in love with two people, but for totally different reasons?

Can someone really be in love with more than one type of lifestyle?
Of course you can, when you actually sit down and think about what it
really is that you love about small towns and big cities. By now you have
a pretty good idea of my passion for living in a small town. If not, I lost
you at "Hello." That is, at the earlier chapter named "Hello, My Name
is Kim and I'm a Small Town Addict." As I discussed earlier, this crazy
relationship I have with my town and other small towns can be described
as love since that means feeling a desire and affection for something.

When, on the other hand, maybe I could more appropriately define
my feelings about big cities as "lust," which I would describe as a powerful
craving or desire for something.

I lust after the tall buildings, the bright lights, and the endless
entertainment venues. And of course, if you know anything about me by
now, I LOVE THE SHOPPING!

Lust can take over your every thought for the short term, but as most
lust relationships go, we tend to go back to the one we truly love. And in
my case, I always go back to my small towns.

In my years of traveling, I've been fortunate to travel to many big cities; however, there is one that seems to steal my heart whenever I go. CHICAGO! In just a couple of days I can get my big city fix of good food, museums, sports, people watching and, oh yeah, did I mention shopping?

By plane, I can be in Chicago in less than an hour, but I prefer driving the less-than-six-hours in the comfort of my own vehicle. This way, I leave when I want, stop where I want, and I am total control of my itinerary. I can also take and bring home as much as I want without fear of overweight luggage. There are also two words that come to mind when deciding to drive. OUTLET SHOPPING. Some of the best outlet stores are located on I-65 en route to Chicago. Sometime I reserve this shopping for the return trip, just in case I did not spend enough money in Chicago.

A little closer to home, I spend a great deal of time in Louisville and Lexington, both less than an hour's drive, and Nashville and Cincinnati, which are just over two hours away.

Driving to Louisville is like putting our vehicles on autopilot. We have been driving there all our lives and it is part of our culture. Considering the fact that Louisville has always been "just up the road," we have never really been lacking for anything. If we didn't have it in our town, we would just jump in our cars and head to Louisville.

If we want the arts, Louisville is considered a cultural Mecca with wonderful theatres, galleries, and music venues. If we want shopping, any type of retail therapy is available. If we want entertainment, there is something there to suit all ages from skate parks and amusement parks to horse racing and riverboat rides. Let's not forget the food—that wonderful array of restaurants that Louisville is so well known for. Vincenzo's and Lily's are my favorites.

Then there are the major state universities in Louisville with University of Louisville and in Lexington with University of Kentucky, which are schools with exceptional reputations and even better sports teams and venues.

If you don't mind driving just a little bit further your options increase. Drive north and Cincinnati is always a favorite for a Bengals or Reds game or maybe shopping at Saks Fifth Avenue. Drive south and you run right into the Country Music Capital in Nashville where any night of the week you can hop from one bar to another downtown and listen to some of the greatest country music around. If you are really lucky, you may score a ticket to a Titans football game.

Our relationships with our big city neighbors are mutually good. We go to the city for things we can't get in our towns, and they come to small town America to enjoy our uniqueness and to "get away to the country."

No one could agree more about this mutual respect than one of my favorite big city leaders, Metro Louisville, Kentucky, Mayor Jerry Abramson. While Mayor Abramson admits the smallest town he has ever lived in is Bloomington, Indiana (Pop. 72,000), where he attended college at Indiana University, he does indeed have small town in his lineage. He is proud to tell you about his great-uncle's dry goods stores in the small towns of Bloomfield and Taylorsville, Kentucky. Abramson could have been born in one of those small towns, since his father, when he got out of the military, was offered the opportunity to run these stores. However, his mother, who was raised in Connecticut, was hoping for a life in a larger city. He says that with a laugh and with the follow-up comment, "in all due respect to small towns."

This "Mayor for Life," as he has been nicknamed by the media because of his more than twenty years running the city, "gets it." He understands that not only do small towns derive much benefit from being geographically close to a large city, but that cities benefit as well because they need patrons for the arts venues, customers at the regional shopping malls, kids at the amusements parks and fans at the university's ball games. Many of those who enjoy all these amenities are from the smaller towns surrounding Louisville.

While big city politics is Mayor Abramson's life, he has an understanding of what goes on in small towns across the Commonwealth of Kentucky. As former president of the Kentucky League of Cities, Abramson has travelled all across the state, and recognizes that small towns outnumber big cities significantly and their problems are similar.

"The issues that we face in communities big or small are mostly the same;

however, in big cities you are usually dealing with a few more zeros to the left side of the decimal point when you talk budgets and funding," he says.

Does he ever find himself envious of some of his counterparts in a small town? He was quick to say, "Oh yes, the bigger the city, the more overwhelming the issues. I think it's the same way that Mayor Daley of Chicago and Mayor Bloomberg of New York are envious of me. They have indicated to me on occasion that handling a city of 700,000 would be easier and maybe even more satisfying, speaking issue related, of course."

Abramson understands and appreciates that not everyone is into a big city lifestyle and that is apparent from the number of "bedroom" communities that surround Louisville. Although people work in Louisville they choose not to live there for numerous reasons, including wanting more land to live on and a more passive lifestyle. The reasons are as different as the towns themselves.

Where you work is not going to decide where you live but the quality of place will. Telecommuting allows you to live anywhere you have a phone line, computer and Internet access. Abramson did say, "Now, if you are a Sarah Jessica Parker and want a *Sex in the City* lifestyle then you need to be in New York City; however, if you decide to have a family and get your life squared away and settled, towns like Bardstown or any of the other great, small towns in Kentucky provide a more solid and comfortable community."

Big cities and small towns can agree that there is one thing that will have to happen to make all these communities successful—they must work as one! Communities must get away from the competition, the "me" versus "you" mentality and work together—that's where the importance of regionalism comes in play. Strength is in numbers. The more people on your team, the stronger you can become. We are not in competition with each other; we are in competition with those in other regions and states who are working to be as strong as us.

When asked what he thought was the sex appeal of a small town, he said, "I love a town square, with vibrant locally-owned businesses wrapped around it and with unique residential experiences. While I love where I am now, I relish that kind of existence."

There is a sort of "best of both worlds" for those of us who live in a small town near a big city. We reap the benefits of all that the city has to offer but we are also able to put our heads in our beds in our small towns where we have chosen to live our lives. Small town residents who live near larger cities have been commuting to work for generations. It is nothing for us to leave at 6 a.m. to be at work at 7 a.m. in Louisville. It's what our grandparents and parents did, and it's what so many are still doing today. It's no big deal, especially compared to what big city commuters contend with each day. Just ask someone who lives in a large metropolitan area how long it takes them to get to work either by car, train or subway.

Small towns near a big city reap many rewards from the successes of those cities. A large turnout for the Kentucky Derby in Louisville every May means towns like Bardstown, Shepherdsville, Elizabethtown and Shelbyville or the Indiana communities across the Ohio River, will get a spillover in hotel rooms and visitors wanting to take a day trip. When large companies like UPS or Ford locate facilities in the city, chances are the surrounding communities will get a trickle-down effect of suppliers.

Unfortunately, we also feel the fallout of their misfortunes as well. The closing of facilities and loss of jobs in the big city ultimately mean the loss of jobs to those who work there and many of them are residents of the region's smaller towns. Personally, I would have to say that a smaller community is only as strong as the larger city that surrounds it. We are closely tied to each other's failures and successes.

Although I prefer my life in a small town, I am in awe of the city. This awe sometimes has me acting a bit odd at times. Is it me or do other people from small towns tend to act differently when they are in a big city? Have you ever dressed a little differently when going out in a big city? Have you ever talked differently? Have you ever tried to put on a big city front, when all along your small town demeanor was showing, like a zipper that is unzipped?

I don't know what it is, but when I am in a big city I try not to look like a fish out of water or too touristy. I think this whole issue may stem back to an experience I had in Los Angeles in the late 1970s when I visited a musician friend who lived there. He was in a band so I knew I would probably be meeting some pretty cool West Coast types. I wanted to make a good impression—I studied fashion magazines for weeks, tore out pictures and took them with me as I shopped for new clothes, and even got a new hair cut for my adventure. I wanted to blend in and not draw attention that I was from another part of the country. I didn't want any Kentucky jokes.

California was amazing and I experienced things I had only seen on television and in the movies. I really thought, "I could live here" and visited UCLA with thoughts of transferring colleges. That was until my ego got a West Coast kick in the butt at a party given for me on my last night. All was going well, until out of nowhere a girl from "the valley" turns to me and says, "So did you have to buy those shoes specifically for this trip?" My naiveté must have been in overdrive that night because not knowing any better I thought she was giving me a compliment . . . until she quickly followed up with the second part of her comment, "I heard you don't wear any in Kentucky."

I was in mid-drink when she said that and just about spit my drink across the room. I was stunned. I didn't know whether to run and hide or to punch her suntanned face. The unfortunate part is, I found out she was serious and not being mean-spirited. It didn't matter how hard I had tried to fit in, my small town Kentucky stereotype showed up at the party with me. So the point of this story is, I don't want people stereotyping those of us in small towns; that's why I try a little too hard to make sure that doesn't happen when I'm visiting a big city.

There are the other times when you just can't help yourself. There are times when small town silly kicks into high gear.

Although no one wants to admit to it because it is often painful and pretty embarrassing, but I often get a break out of being what's known as STG. No, not STD (where was your mind going?), but STG—"SMALL TOWN GIRL." STG is what happens to you when you do something, see something, or in my case buy something, that makes it apparent you are not from the city. As with other outbreaks, like a pimple or a rash, STGs come at the most inopportune time, usually when I am in a big city, trying to fit in.

Case in point, the time I bought my one and only authentic Louis Vuitton purse. I say authentic because I did own my share of fake ones, you know the ones you buy in New York City, in the dark alley, in the bottom of a black garbage bag from someone you don't know. Do you think you would ever go into a dark alley, in New York City with a man you don't know, unless it was to buy a knock-off designer purse? Hell No! But a Louis Vuitton knockoff, I would have gotten in a car and driven away with him, if he had told me he had Louis Vuitton purses at his house.

STG OUTBREAK!!!

You know there has to be a good story to go along with the first-ever purchase of a real, way too expensive, Louis Vuitton handbag. And here's mine.

For about a week, I had been bad—very bad. In my spare time, I would get on the Internet and browse those sites, you know them, the ones that tease you first and then lure you in slowly. I was obsessed. Every day, I would go back to this same site over and over, four, and five maybe six times a day. I couldn't get enough of it. There it was sitting right in front of me. It was so close I could almost touch it. And have it I would. I had been on the official Louis Vuitton website and lusting after the most beautiful Louis Vuitton handbag you have ever seen.

My partner in crime in this spending offense would be my oldest daughter, Erin, whom I convinced on a moment's notice to drive with me, more than two hours, to the nearest Louis Vuitton store in Saks Fifth

Avenue in Cincinnati. Taking off for the big cities are no big deal for my daughters. Erin spends about a weekend every other month in Las Vegas with her B.F.F. Jess who moved there after college. My youngest, Meg, is so adventurous, when most of her friends were going to Florida for spring break, she and two friends spent a week in London and Paris seeing the sights and experiencing European fashion. So popping off to Cincinnati was like a drive to the corner drug store for Erin.

One hour later we are on Interstate 75 heading to Cincinnati. Not really knowing how to get to the Saks Fifth Avenue, I called my friend Lisa, a connoisseur of everything Louis and who lived near Cincy. She would play the role of consultant for this journey. She told us how to get downtown to the store from the interstate and what to look for when we got there.

This was one of the most spontaneous purchase adventures I had ever been on.

At 6 p.m. we arrived in Cincinnati. I had butterflies in my stomach crossing the street and walking into the store. I didn't want to seem over anxious so I wandered through some of the other purse areas first. Dolce and Gabbana, Michael Kors and Chanel. I saw some unbelievably gorgeous purses, but I knew where my heart was. After taking a deep breath, I walked through the glass doors and into what I think heaven might look like one of these days. Display after display of Louis. But I was there for only one, the "it" bag, The Louis Vuitton Palermo bag. Okay, I hadn't driven all this way, to just pick it up and go, I was going to savor this moment and make it last. I asked my Louis assistant, a really sweet guy if I could pick up the bags. He looked at the other assistant, giggled for a second and said "of course."

STG outbreak.

With that said, I went through the store fondling every bag. Like a beauty pageant final, I had him line three of them up for me on the counter. I walked about the table looking at them from all angles and trying them all on again. I couldn't have been more excited if I was test-driving a new car.

Knowing they were closing in less than an hour, I had to make a decision. But this was a fashion altering experience for me, and I wanted to take my time. Then all of the sudden, words involuntarily came out of my mouth; I said, "I'll take the biggest one."

Oh, my god! Did I just say that? Did that just come out of my mouth? Apparently so, because my assistant starting clapping his hands in excitement as if his sister had just won the beauty pageant. Once his excitement settled he asked, "Would you like me to put that in a box for you?" Still a bit stunned from my monumental decision, my daughter answered for me, "Yes, she would."

After putting my new purse in a huge brown Louis Vuitton Box, tying it with a piece of real leather and then placing it in a beautiful Louis Vuitton shopping bag, I realized that the box and bag presentation probably cost more than any purse I owned before today. I know you are just dying for me to tell you how much it cost? Right? Wrong! Just like our weight, it's something girls just don't talk about.

When we left the store, Erin and I decided to walk up and down the streets of downtown Cincinnati for a few moments with the Louis Vuitton bag for all to see and hopefully gawk at. When we got back to the car, we took turns, taking pictures with our phones of each other holding the bag.

That was the biggest STG outbreak of the day.

SMALL TOWN *Sexy*

is knowing that it's okay to be envious of those bigger than you,

because chances are they are envious of you as well.

"Good things come in small packages."

—*Unknown Author*

chapter eleven

More Characters than Disney

A wise man by the name of Tom Isaac once told me, "Characters are the texture of the community." And like so many pieces of wisdom he has instilled in me over the years, I know he is absolutely right.

I use the term "character" very affectionately to describe the special individuals in our communities. These individuals possess distinctive and interesting personalities and bring a sort of unique "color" to the community where they live. You know them and probably see them quite often, because they are usually some of the more visible citizens in our towns. They may be those funny retired gentleman who sit on a bench watching the world go by as they talk about the "good old days." Or they may be the ones that attend every government meeting fighting for their right to speak on the issue of the day, whether it be allowing alcohol sales on Sunday, taking the trees out of the downtown, or how to regulate stray dogs. They have an opinion and it is going to be heard.

I will bet you ten bucks that as soon as I mentioned the word "character" you immediately got an image in your mind of at least one in your community. You know the ones, and you see them often, because in many cases they are usually very friendly, do odd jobs for people and often we only know them by their first name or maybe just a nickname.

You trust them, although you really don't know them very well. They just seem so darn likable. These characters are our television show equivalents of Larry, Darryl and his other brother Darryl, or our Mr. Haney, or maybe more recent comparison would be Wilson from *Home Improvement* or Kramer from *Seinfeld*—all very colorful and lovable.

One of Bardstown's most well-known and visible characters is Walter. He is one of my favorites.

Walter is a one-armed gentle giant of a man who can usually be found sitting with his friends in our downtown Court Square waiting to do some work for our local business people. Walter is rarely by himself. He is usually with his bicycle-riding group of friends.

Not many people really know Walter though they may pass him every day on the sidewalk. I doubt that very few even know how Walter lost his arm. I know the story because Walter was featured in the 2003 *Mountain Workshop Book*, a project of the Western Kentucky University Journalism Department. They wanted to feature our grassroots folk and Walter ended up as a chapter.

When Walter was eighteen years old he was helping out on a farm, when working with a hay bale, he was suddenly knocked to the ground and run over by a wagon. Doctors were forced to amputate his right arm about halfway between his elbow and shoulder. However, to watch Walter work, you'd never know he is missing a limb. He can outwork just about anyone. He is trusted by many of our local business people who hire him to sweep, clean windows, and take out trash. Walter also has a list of clients who hire him to mow their yards.

Walter is in town when I get there every morning and there when I leave. I can always count on him to be my first "good morning" of the day.

*O*ver the years, Tom Isaac has probably seen more than his share of characters, due to his extensive background in radio and television broadcasting in small towns. As news director for PLG TV-13

in Bardstown, he is known as "the man who is everywhere" because, as you must realize, in small town media, you have to be everywhere. And if the fair pageant committee wants you to cover their queen contest you are there until that winner is crowned. And small town sports, well, that's just a different animal all its own. Undoubtedly, trying to fairly cover three high schools and the multitude of sports they have is probably one of the biggest challenges of small town TV, radio or newspaper.

With a camera by his side, like another appendage, Tom travels all over our county chasing the news of the day and getting back just in time to write the stories, type out his script, and record it for the 6 p.m. airing. Isaac is as recognizable and respected in Nelson County as Matt Lauer is in New York.

I never really thought about it before, but Tom fits the profile of a character in our community. He is visible, colorful, interesting, and uniquely honest. He doesn't look like your typical nightly newscaster. As a matter of fact, he resembles one of my former college professors. And he's smart. I don't mean rocket-science smart, I mean well-read and down-to-earth smart. More importantly, Tom is trustworthy and believable. If he were to report on one of his broadcasts that the sky was going to fall at 5 p.m. that evening, everyone would be buying shovels and digging shelters by 4 p.m.

Like Dr. Phil knows relationships, Tom and I both know characters because we have had our share of meeting and interviewing them over our extensive careers in broadcasting. While some of these characters were the unfortunate ones who made the nightly newscast due to "unforseen circumstances," my favorite characters were the ones I met during the seven-year run of my *On Location* television program. During these years, I met and interviewed some of the most interesting and fascinating small town characters who have left a lasting impression on me with their sometimes humorous, sometimes heartbreaking, but always inspiring stories.

On one memorable show, I interviewed Mayor Gus Wilson and we talked about his lifetime as a small town mayor, and the day that Pres. Jimmy Carter came to town.

I took our viewers on a tour of our underground cave system. Despite the fact that I am claustrophobic, this was a real treat for the viewers.

Bardstown resident Catherine Conner, a former Washington socialite and youngest national Democratic Committee Chairwoman, spoke to me from her wheelchair in the garden of her nursing home. She had a résumé that read like Washington royalty.

I interviewed country music stars, met families who raised buffalo, rode a horse like I was in the Kentucky Derby, and featured several high school and college sports standouts from Nelson County. I have been on the water, in the air, and every place in between for interviews. There was laughter through interviews and many a tear shed off camera.

On Location was the small town equivalent of *60 Minutes,* The CBS *Sunday Morning* program and the Travel Channel programs all rolled into one. Our audience loved getting a glimpse into the lives of these characters, many of whom they never knew even existed.

Towns without characters would be very dull.

Although most small towns have evolved from the Mayberry style of life, one thing will never change. All towns do have their share of characters. They may not be the Barneys or the Otises of the world, but they are colorful characters nonetheless and sometimes just as loveable.

I guess you could say that some small towns have more characters than Disney.

We all grew up with the likes of Mickey Mouse and Donald Duck, adorable Disney characters that we all loved and could relate to in some way, and we considered them our best friends as we watched them on television. Nobody does it better than Disney in sparking the imagination in all of us.

After mastering the art of creativity with the likes of Disney World and Disney Land, a few years ago, Disney embarked on yet another former of magical and creative development.

That magic is known as the town of Celebration, Florida. In 2000 the population was estimated at 2,736, give or take a few characters of their own. However, they say Celebration has now grown to around 10,000 residents.

Celebration is famously known as the town that Disney designed and built as the iconic "perfect small town."

At this point you may be thinking to yourself, how does this segue from characters, to a town that Disney built, all fit into *Small Town Sexy*. It's simple. As I said before, people who live in small towns are as different as the types of small towns that exist in America to today. You do not have to be in rural America to live in a small town. Small communities are scattered throughout the country. They may be villages or hamlets within larger cities; some may even consider the neighborhoods of suburbia to be like small communities in themselves.

Or you can be even be more unique and reside in Celebration, a small town, outside a large city and more distinctive, outside the gates of the Magic Kingdom at Disney World.

But don't be mistaken, Celebration is not home to Mickey Mouse or Donald Duck; it is a master planned community developed in 1996. The first time I went to Celebration I was filled with awe, as well as envy, because it was my opinion that the town's master planners took the best-of-the-best of towns all across the country, and put them together in one ideal town and, voila—Celebration!

When you are there, don't ask the residents how much they get paid to portray their role as residents of this town. These residents are real people with real jobs, real kids and real dogs.

Teddy Benson, Celebration resident and volunteer tech-head, (he is a software engineer in Celebration) laughs when he tells me about the many times that visitors have asked him how much he got paid to work as a character in this town. He describes the time several Japanese visitors stood on his sidewalk and videotaped him mowing his lawn. Then there was the one older couple who stopped to ask where the rides were located in this part of the park.

A Celebration resident since 1997, Benson loves his life there. He enjoys saying that Celebration probably has more characters than the average town just because of the fact that it is a Disney town and because of the fascinating people from people all over the world who want to live there.

Benson and his wife moved to Celebration from Boca Raton, Florida, in 1997—when they agreed it was time to start a family in a community where neighbors and family values were part of the cornerstones of its existence. In describing what Disney was looking for in designing this town, Benson says he thinks the developers were trying to gather the essence of a perfect town and encompass as much of that as they could. They then sat down and said okay, now let's make a ten-year plan of what this small town could be from start to finish.

The town is idyllic. From its diverse architecture design on its houses, to its well-maintained parks and boardwalks, everything in its villages are laid out with a reason and a plan. And of course, you have to know that Celebration is using technology in a wonderfully innovative way. The town is very on-line prolific and operates its own internal website that is literally walked upon daily, and for more in-tuned residents, on an hourly basis. Even its name is so Disneylike—"The Front Porch." The site is log-in protected and is a daily on-line newspaper that provides residents details of what is going on, a list of events, minutes of committee meetings, an open forum for residents to sell things, and the ability to hobnob with other residents in a virtual front porch atmosphere.

"It's not perfect," Benson says. "Not unlike any other small towns and the problems they suffer through, Celebration does have its share of flaws and growing pains. Because it's one of the first communities of its type, it is learning to keep up with ever-changing technology needs. We pride ourselves in being leaders in community technology and we are going to have to work hard to continue to invest in facilities as technology changes."

Another issue is the lack of shopping amenities. Residents will talk about leaving the "bubble," or the "little island," if you will, which are the limits of the town. Because Disney did not want to lose that small town vision, they do not allow mainstream branded stores to locate in the town in fear that the small town effect would be destroyed. That has been an issue for some of the town folk who want to buy a book, or go to a department store. Not unlike most any small town, you have to leave town to do that.

And as far as the characters in his own town, Benson loves talking about local doctor who plays Uncle Sam each year and leads the Fourth of July Parade, or the "Java Joes" who religiously meet for coffee at Starbucks at 7:30 a.m. sharp. He laughs when he talks about the residents who own their own Neighborhood Electronic Vehicle (NEV), an upscale and elaborate type of golf cart, and who decal and paint them to reflect their style. This includes an older lady who does her daily "walk" with her dog, from the comfort of her NEV designed like a 1950s Rolls Royce. Benson said people might put him in that same character category since he is the guy who rides his Segway to and from work each day.

Benson is passionate when he emphasizes that Celebration is a real-life, living and breathing small town unlike the fabricated ones just up the road in the Magic Kingdom. He said the people, the amount of pride and conscious effort that residents put into the town make it a great place to live.

SMALL TOWN *Sexy*

is about embracing the fact that people who live in small towns

are as different as the towns themselves.

"Problems can be opportunities
when the right people come together."
—Robert Redford

chapter twelve

THEY'RE JUST NOT THAT INTO YOU

Are you kidding me? What do you mean, "They're just not that into you?" What's "not to be into" about small town life? The first time I heard someone say that they could never live in a small town I thought it was a joke and expected that *Candid Camera* guy to jump out of the bushes with a camera pointed in my face. It's ridiculous, right?

As much as it pains me to do this, I have to share a dirty little secret that I have been hiding from you this entire book:

SMALL TOWNS ARE NOT FOR EVERYONE.

Ouch! That hurt like a knife in the heart. But it needed to be said. Right now, right here and before we go any further. It's critical to this particularly painful chapter in the book.

For you *Sex in the City* fans, and you proudly know who you are (me included), you might remember one of my favorite episodes of that television series. It's where the ladies have just met Carrie's new boyfriend, Berger, and they are all sitting at a restaurant talking when Miranda tells them about a date she had where the guy didn't want to come up to her apartment afterwards. She asks Berger to give a male analysis of her date's behavior. Knowing nothing good can come out of anything he could say, he was hesitant to give a reply. Finally those six harsh words come out of his mouth, "He's just not that into you." The girls are stunned. No, it couldn't possibly be that. It must have been that the guy had to get up early and work the next day. Sure, that's it—any way to rationalize and avoid the hard-core truth, that maybe, just maybe, he's right.

We have all played this same scenario out in our heads before, sometimes relating it to a personal situation, and sometimes as it relates to a work issue. I have had both, and was always hard pressed to understand why? Why are they not into me, my company or maybe my community? I always conceded that it had to be something wrong with them—maybe a mental imbalance that prevents them from making the right decisions.

They are like the couple assessing towns to live in, the group tour leader looking for destinations for their church group. There was the company that I wined and dined for two days in hopes they would locate their newest manufacturing operations here. Why didn't they call back? Don't they know we were named as one of the *1000 Places to See Before You Die*? Are you kidding me? What's not to like?

Apparently, a lot in some people's eyes. I have heard it all:

"It's a cute little town, but there is not enough here to keep me entertained." (I think they ended up moving to Las Vegas.)

"I don't cook and I eat out every night. There are not enough restaurants and the variety sucks." (Sorry, but that was an actual quote. Kind of glad he didn't move here with that attitude.)

"I am used to staying to myself and I don't like people in my business." (They need to find a quiet island somewhere in the Pacific.)

"There are not enough people who live here to make our business successful." (I have heard this several times from larger national companies—just give us time, new people are moving in every day.)

And then the one that I hear while wearing my economic development hat, and the most dreaded comment that I always take issue with:

"We need a smart and skilled workforce and the numbers don't work here."

This is the one excuse I could sit and intelligently debate for days, because if you haven't done your homework, it tends to be no more than a perception issue about small town workers. No, not all of our people are college or even high school grads, and no, they don't all have technical training (although a good number of them do). But what they do have is good old-fashioned small town smarts. It's a work ethic that is so admirable in small towns everywhere.

Never underestimate the value of "small town smarts." This is your getting-back-to-basics figure-it-out and-get-things-done mentality. Small town workers may not always be the ones inventing the next great technology or developing a new kind of fuel, but being more isolated from a larger city has played a huge role in making small towns and their people self-sufficient.

I have discovered by working as what I sometimes refer to as a "recruiter," one of my biggest challenges is overcoming a preconceived perception of we are in small town America. A company or individual may not be "into you" because they don't know any better. They may not have the latest facts and figures for your town and may be working off of outdated research. Information about our communities including population, home prices, and unemployment rates are called our "demographics." Communities can get eliminated from projects for not having the right information at the right time. If you don't have this information, GET IT! It's like having that right tool in your toolbox when you are ready to work.

Most state economic development agencies have this profile information on the communities in their state. Pull it together in a manageable form and have it on hand, and even better, on your website for everyone to access. Knowledge is important and this information can answer a lot of questions: "Yes, we do have a well-educated workforce; yes, we do have training programs in place; and yes, the cost of living is lower than most places in the U.S."

But in the inspiring words of the great redneck comedian, Larry the Cable Guy, it takes more than just information to "Git-R-Done." It takes relationships with people outside your own "bubble" to spread the word about what you have to offer.

I am a true believer in relationships. Good relationships are the key to happiness in our personal lives, and the relationships we form in our business lives are key to much of our success. There is a big old world outside the gates of our small town. To grow we must open these gates and form partnerships and get the word out to a larger audience. I have great small town partners in my region. It's not so much about being in competition with your neighboring county anymore as it is about promoting your entire region as a great place to do business.

One of my regional partners is Bob Fouts. He is my counterpart in neighboring Bullitt County, which has become one of the fastest growing areas for economic development in Kentucky. It has something all economic developers want—Interstate 65 running right smack down the middle of the county with development potential on each side.

Bob is retired from the Kentucky Cabinet for Economic Development and has been an economic development mentor for many of this field. Bob is not only well connected, but is highly respected, not only for the knowledge he possesses, but for the mild mannerly way in which he does business. I tease Bob when we are at functions together, and tell him that I plan to stay close because he seems to be a magnet for deals. During a Kentucky Association for Economic Development annual conference in Northern Kentucky, I did stay close and as the old saying goes, "I was in the right place, at the right time," and that place was right next to Bob.

While he and I were standing in the hallway talking about a session that had just finished, he saw two gentlemen walking our way and told me he wanted to introduce me to these guys who could be very important to me in the future. At that time, however, neither of us had a clue that this brief introduction would lead so quickly to a very prosperous relationship.

Tom Sims and Doug Butcher are part of the Industrial Properties team with the national real estate firm of CB Richard Ellis (CBRE). Based out of Louisville, Kentucky, these guys and their team have been responsible for millions of dollars worth of industrial real estate deals in Kentucky and Indiana. Corporations that don't have the time or the real estate knowledge are hiring firms like CBRE with the global experience and resources available to assist in the site selection process.

It was a great introduction. These guys were genuine and seemed sincerely interested in what I was doing in Bardstown and wanted to learn more.

From that moment, a prosperous business relationship was formed and I was fortunate to have two new good friends. To condense the next year's worth of events, that initial meeting resulted in a visit by Tom and Doug to Bardstown for a whirl-wind tour of my community. Fast forward a couple of months, when Tom was back in Bardstown, this time on a site selection visit with a national company. There were several more visits by this company over the next few months.

This story has a happy ending: a national company that I told you about earlier, Flowers Foods of Thomasville, Georgia, eventually selected Bardstown as the location of their newest state-of-the-art bread and bun facility. This success story was a direct result of a relationship that was formed in Northern Kentucky that day. That introduction to the CBRE guys turned out to be one of the most important ones of my career.

Tom and Doug were enlightening about the site selection process and how small towns fare in this very competitive business. They explained that a company may not be "into you" as a place to do business, because they don't know enough about you to make an informed decision. They added, however, that there is another factor that small towns cannot get away from and it's what we have been talking about the entire chapter, "perception."

I needed to learn more about these "perceptions" and what we could do as small towns to overcome these negative influences. So months after we did the Flowers Foods deal, I went back to CBRE to find out what it takes for us to get away from small town stereotypes. I asked Doug to help me in my quest.

Let me tell you a little about Doug Butcher. He is one of those guys that cause you to pay attention. He has a confidence without being arrogant and intelligence without talking over your head. His knowledge of real estate is apparent and you feel a built-in trust knowing that he has your best interest at heart. Of course, he wants to do a deal, but I am confident in knowing that he also wants to do something that will ultimately benefit my community. CBRE, in the past couple of years, has successfully done business in small towns like Bardstown, Georgetown and Elizabethtown, Kentucky, and Corydon, Indiana. So they have experience in both cities and small towns and know there are differences in the way clients view the size of a community.

Not all companies are into small towns as a place to do business (shame on them) and some of them will probably never take a look at a town under 20,000 or sometimes even 50,000 people. Butcher says that there are typically a number of factors in choosing a small town for a company location, but usually it will come down to some type of cost savings. "Each prospect will have several issues that are very important to them that drive their motives, including wages, employee/workforce base, utility rates, and proximity to a client or to their customers. And then of course, they may want a certain parameter of education or skill level in the community."

On the positive side, he said there is certainly the attraction of looking at small towns, not only for the incentives, but being thought of as a "big fish in a small pond." "Some of these prospects realize that they will receive special treatment from local officials and the community when they locate to a small town and they find that appealing as long as it makes logistical sense to reach their clients and customers. A company often likes being the brand of the community."

Now, getting back to the "just not into you" factors. Doug agrees that unless towns have the power to move a major highway or interstate to their communities that there are projects that will never take a look. Transportation is a huge investment, and companies look for ways to lessen their expenses. And what about towns that have no airport? Unless they have the funds to make this investment, there is another group of projects they will never see.

Bottom-line, what can small towns do to make themselves more attractive to companies outside of building an airport or winning the go-ahead for an interstate highway? Butcher says small towns have the ability to react quickly to the needs of a prospect or existing client and this is very appealing. He adds that small towns also have the ability to streamline any processes such as incentives and construction issues—having plans in place to address concerns like road construction, power, workforce, Internet and other infrastructure needs. Of course, let's not forget, the incentives. That's one little carrot that many communities still have. These might be as simple as a reduction in land prices, tax abatements, or assistance with infrastructure needs. In small towns, because there are fewer people involved in the decision making process, permits and incentive packages can be approved quickly. This is *Small Town Sexy* to most companies.

In his years of working with small towns and their community leaders, Butcher says he has found these communities to be appealing and alluring in their own unique ways. "The appeal of knowing a large percentage of the people, gaining intimate attention, and the thought of playing a large role in a small community are all very attractive. Generally people slow down in a smaller town and take the time to talk and discuss any needs or concerns." And finally, and maybe more importantly, he added that there is the loyalty of local citizens in a small town that is hard to find anywhere else. There is nothing more enticing than that and it doesn't cost you a cent.

*I*f you were not raised in a small town and never had an opportunity to experience life here, you may at times find yourself comparing it to visiting a foreign country. I say that with all due respect to my international clients and friends. Depending on what part of the country you are from, not only will small town culture be a bit different, but the language maybe challenging as well. And if you are from the "real big city," the anonymity that is so appealing in a large place has been substituted for what I like to describe as a "fish bowl" world. Large cities are bustling with hundreds of thousands or even millions of people and you don't have to worry about making eye contact or speaking to those you pass on the street. Too many people going in too many directions to be able to relate in that sort of way. What you find in a small town is that if you don't make eye contact and you don't speak, you are either snobby or just plain rude.

The difference in big city/small town language made national headlines on an episode of *American Idol*. During a qualifying round in Louisville, Kentucky, a good ol' boy from Cox's Creek, Kentucky (which, by the way, is just outside of my hometown) had sung a George Jones song. Not feeling he was "Idol" quality, he did not get the "yes" from all three judges he needed to continue on to the next round and was excused. On his way off the stage, as he was saying his goodbyes, he said to them:

"Y'all be careful."

A dazed and confused Judge Paula Abdul looked up and said, "Did he just threaten us?"

Maybe in "Big City America" this same sentence might have a more threatening meaning like "you better watch your back." But here in the South, that is a simple phrase that can be translated to mean, "Have a good trip back," "Be safe," or hey—let me go out on a limb here—maybe it meant, "be careful." That's what my Mom would lovingly say to me just about every time I would leave the house.

This one little phrase made him an overnight sensation on the Internet and brought a lot of attention to the difference in cultures that exists in our country today.

And then there's the gossip. The not-so-accurate-tabloid-like information passed down from person to person that travels faster than the bullet train in Japan. Do we know people's business in small towns?

Yep!

Is that ever going to change?

Nope!

It's a small town and when stuff happens you are going to know about it. While you are sitting getting your haircut or having a cup of coffee at the local diner, you are going to talk. However, they are talking at Starbucks in New York City about someone in their circle of acquaintances. No matter how big the town, the more diluted it seems. This is something in small towns that will never change, so we will politely suggest you just deal with it.

∽∽∽

*N*ot everyone moves to small town America because they want to and we know many come "kickin' and screamin'." Nonetheless, they are forced to live here because of a job transfer, a family obligation, or a slew of other reasons. We can spot these "newbies" a mile away and in our town it is our "mission" to win these people over in the ways of small town life. It's not that we show up with plates of cookies each day, or offer to walk their dogs while they are at work; we just invite them to join in and be part of what makes this lifestyle so attractive. You have to know us to love us, and getting involved puts you face-to-face with people who love small town life and sometimes it has been known to rub off.

I have seen the biggest of naysayers—those I never thought we could convert to loving small town life—volunteer to sell burgers at our local events and be the first to be in line at a concert in the park.

I am pretty confident that not all your neighbors will greet you with a pitcher of ice tea over the backyard fence and chances are pretty slim that you can walk to the corner newspaper stand and pick up a *New York Times* or *Wall Street Journal*. I am pretty confident that you would be hard-pressed to find a corner newspaper stand. However, you can pick up a copy of the local newspaper and see what is happening in your own back yard—and there's always the public library somewhere close by. Maybe you want to know where they are giving free flu shots that week, what pets are up for adoption at the local Humane Society and how the hometown team fared in the district basketball tournament.

If you are looking for a life filled with wandering through galleries full of famous works of art, or a venue that hosts major Broadway productions, then you are not going to be content in small town America. But what you are going to enjoy are concerts in the park, storefronts filled with local works of art, numerous high school drama productions, and wonderful festivals showcasing the amazing craftsmen of the area. These are those great hometown happenings that are the life of small towns.

Problems? Sure we have our own version of big-city-like problems, like traffic and noise for instance. Our traffic downtown comes to a crawl when you get behind "Jonesie" giving one of his special tours in his fully-restored horse and carriage through our tree-lined streets of the Historic District. Or maybe you got behind Dan, driving the Heaven Hill Trolley, which travels slowly as its passes our historic sites and takes passengers to the distillery for a "taste" of our history. If you are in the country, be watchful of the horseback riders out for a Sunday ride across the back roads of the county, or the cattle that may be making their way to the field on the other side of the road. Then there is the noise; the loud sounds of music coming from the City Park during a Friday night concert featuring the Ft. Knox Army Band or maybe one our own homegrown bands entertaining hundreds of people in the Farmers Market Pavilion downtown.

Yes, life is pretty good in small towns all across the country. Although we enjoy where we are, there does come the time that we need a little more. Sometimes, a road trip to where life's a bit faster, more lively, and with endless options of things to fill that need. Big city excitement is something we save for special times and where we try to cram seven days worth of fun into only three. Typically, I am glad when the trip ends, because I have exhausted myself so much trying to shop in every store, eat in every restaurant and visit everything worth seeing.

My fiftieth birthday was one of these special occasions that merited celebrating in a big city way.

There needed to be good food, great shopping and exciting things to do. But most importantly, it had to include my good friends, Julie Wilson Garrett and Jane Roby. Cue the "sunshine girls"—an affectionate name we gave ourselves.

It was during a night of good white wine and smooth Bardstown bourbon that we decided my fiftieth had to include a trip to the city. Not just any city. There was no discussion, no debate. It had to be Chicago! Can you say "Girls Trip?"

I shared earlier my "What I Love About Chicago" list, which are all still important. However on this trip, only one item on the list was relevant: THE SHOPPING. The bevy of designer stores that I only get a taste of at home in fashion magazines. When I die, just cremate me and scatter my ashes over the Louis Vuitton store because I will then know that I am in heaven.

A trip to Chicago is never complete without a visit to my friends, Joan and Jim Conway. These are my big city friends with small town charm, friendliness and attitude. They are like your neighbors next door so I swear they must have been small town folk in another life. They are a couple you become instant friends with.

So here I was going to Chicago for my momentous occasion, and I knew it wouldn't be complete without the company of Joan and Jim. After a glass to wine at their home to toast the beginning of this celebration, they informed us that they would be taking us to their favorite restaurant, Kinzie Chophouse, located in the River North neighborhood only a short train ride from their home.

I loved Kinzie's the moment I walked in the door. It had a sophisticated air about it, without the pretense and it was a place you immediately felt comfortable. It was apparent that this restaurant was a local favorite by the fact that the patrons knew the staff by name and vice versa. We were seated in this great oversized leather booth in the corner of the bar, perfectly situated where you could see everyone there. It was the perfect setting for a perfect evening with friends.

As impressive as the ambiance at Kinzie's, so was its owner, Susan Frasca. She stopped by our table to say hello to Joan and Jim and make sure they were coming to her wine tasting the following day. After being introduced and talking for only a few minutes, I could see why the restaurant was so successful. She was as business savvy as she was beautiful. The fact that she sent champagne to our table, in honor of my birthday, endeared me to her and her restaurant forever. The celebration in the big city was off to a good start.

I must say for a moment the "green" in me came out and I felt a bit envious of my Chicago friends and their life there. This was an exciting city where you can hop on a train and eat at a different restaurant every night of the year, experience the culture and sophistication of the city and let's not forget, walk into Louis Vuitton every day and fondle the merchandise. For a moment I thought to myself, I could be converted. It only took a split second for me to remember my five-minute drive to work and my wonderful "window to the world" in my office to realize where my true love lies. This however, for the night, would be my "lust."

As we finished dinner and were making our way out of the bar, we stopped to meet Joan's sister, Jude, and her friend, Nancy. Jim, knowing that I was writing a book, had decided to be my newly-acquired agent, and was passing my business cards out to anyone who would take one. He thought Nancy and I should meet because we had a couple of things in common. The first is that she is a published author and has been very successful with the books she has written. Secondly, this former Chicago resident had converted to life in small town America.

Very intrigued, we started talking. It only took a couple of minutes to know that if Nancy and I had lived closer, we would become good friends. We had so many things parallel in our lives and so much to talk about. Since I had to leave to continue the birthday celebration, Nancy and I exchanged e-mail addresses and committed to keeping in touch.

I tell this story about the trip to Chicago and my encounter with Nancy, because I have discovered this lifelong big-city girl is now a converted small town enthusiast who has traded her heels for boots and is living as a full-time resident of Eagle River, Wisconsin (Pop. 1,443).

Nancy Diepenbrock is proud to tell you that one of her neighbors in Eagle River affectionately refers to her as "Mountain Woman." Living on her own in the Northwoods of Wisconsin, near the Michigan border, Diepenbrock is a very self-sufficient woman, taking care of her own home, acreage and horses. She owns her own set of tools, including a very sharp chain saw.

Nancy exudes confidence when you talk to her even though she will admit to you that she really didn't expect to be living there alone at this point in her life. But she is quick to tell you that right now, she would live nowhere else.

A registered nurse and an author of critical care nursing books,

Diepenbrock was born and raised in Chicago, but thinks she is a small town girl born in a big city. "I always enjoyed visiting my relatives who lived on a farm and I couldn't wait to be around the cows and chickens. I remember, on every gift-giving occasion, I was constantly begging my parents to buy me a pony. While I knew that I was physically a product of the city, to some degree, country has always been in my soul."

While living in the city, Diepenbrock and her husband decided they would buy a second home that would become their weekend retreat on a lake. After looking at various locations, they selected a beautiful lake house on Pine Island, a place she loves to call her "little chunk of heaven." She never expected that this weekend retreat would become her full-time home after a separation and eventual divorce in 2003. Now, six years later, Eagle River is still her home.

"It does take a special person to make the adjustment from living in the big city most of your life to the small town life, but I feel like I have adjusted just fine." She explains that the one key to making this transition from life in a big exciting city, to life in the slower pace of small town America is being able to use the Internet to stay in touch with "civilization."

"I really miss the news. I only get three TV stations; I don't get CNN, and refuse to cave into satellite television. We don't get a daily newspaper, so I have to rely on my computer to find out what's going on in the news."

There are other differences in her life, including trading dressing up and going to restaurants for putting on her jeans and going to the local fish fry. Her "Taste of Chicago" has been replaced by the "Taste of Eagle River," which she admits is pretty hokey but also very quaint. There is no Chicago Symphony, but Eagle River does have a performing arts series at the local high school.

There are some other differences in big city versus small town life. In small towns, you learn to be more trusting of strangers.

One day as she was driving home from town she turned onto her roadway that was a couple miles long. While driving, she came upon two men, apparently hunters, with rifles slung over their shoulders. Knowing that hunting was not allowed in that area, she pulled her car over, rolled down her window and asked, "Are you guys lost or something?" (Strange men and guns—I told you she was confident.) They replied that they got turned around somehow and were looking for where they parked their truck. After telling her where they thought they parked, she offered these strangers (with rifles and ammunition) a ride to their truck.

(Let me write this once more so you can understand, two strangers, two rifles with ammunition, in the woods and these men are now alone with her in her truck.)

Of course, you know it all worked out just fine and they were so appreciative they sent her a note and small ornament at Christmas.

To Diepenbrock this was nothing out of the ordinary. "You know, it's just what we do out here in the woods. We are very trusting of people and most everyone is very honest and legitimate," she mused. She did laugh for a minute and admit had that same scenario happened in Chicago, she would have kept on driving.

I am so happy that life is good for this big city girl who has developed a love of small town America.

"I love the seasons and I even love the snow and all the activities that surround winter. I love when the grass is green, the flowers bloom and the eagles take flight. I walk in the woods with my dogs and have eight miles of trails out my back door. I can actually say, I live where others vacation."

In a chapter titled "They're Just Not That into You," I would be remiss, and probably a little biased, if I did not spend at least a few paragraphs talking about the not-so-sexy side of small towns and rural America. As much as I love and preach its wonders, it is not Christmas every day here.

Just like age takes its toll on us, there is a similarity of what the aging process does to a community. As a town ages it takes on other traits and characteristics that changes the way we remember it looking when we were young. There may be more residential areas and less farmland, and there may be growth that has taken the center of commerce away from the heart of the downtown and moved it to the outskirts of town. Some of the beautiful buildings we remember, have aged to a state of disrepair, while others have been torn down altogether with a new, more modern structure taking its place.

Small towns have prided themselves in attempting to be as progressive as possible. However, some of the actions these communities have taken changed the landscape of their towns.

I will not debate the Wal-Mart, Kmart or other big box store effects on small towns because I have not found a great consensus among the population of small towns. There are residents who think these stores are the devil disguised in a big box who forced the Mom and Pop businesses to close. Others praise them as being the only place in their communities that you can get anything, thus eliminating the need to drive to a larger community nearby. Some of these businesses that survived the arrival of these stores decided not to compete and changed their inventory or increased their customer service options. Not all stores are able to compete. Others hope that customer loyalty will continue to keep them in business.

By-passes, in my opinion, are the necessary evils of a small town. As a little girl, I used to love driving through all the small towns on vacation. You were actually able to see the heart and soul of a community as these highways took you down their main streets. Today, towns look for funds to help construct new by-passes hoping to re-route truck traffic away and ease congestion of the downtown area. I agree that this is beneficial for large truck traffic looking to avoid the narrow highways and traffic signals of a downtown. This may even improve the area's ambiance. What I don't agree on is that it is always beneficial to the businesses missing out on potential customers. The re-routing of traffic can cause adverse effects on the businesses downtown and the impact of this can be significant. Not only is the truck traffic diverted, but so is the local traffic, as well as of those traveling the state roadways enjoying the communities these roadways led them through. Unless you pay particular attention to signage, by-passes can cause you to totally sidestep the essence of the community, which is usually its downtown.

When surveying people about changes in a small town, the one issue that I could get almost total consensus on was school consolidation. For those who lived life before the smaller schools were merged into county systems, they agree that this movement took the life right out of many small towns and changed the relationships that parents had with the teachers. In so many communities, the schools were the one common denominator in bringing a town together and residents had a sense of ownership in their local schools. The town would be empty on a Friday night because everyone was at the school gym for a basketball game.

It gave us camaraderie as a community. I understand the economics of this action, but I don't have to like it.

An issue that is debated by all successful small towns is the growth factor. Not just any growth, but smart growth. Small towns can live long and prosper as long as their economy flourishes and their leaders monitor where this growth takes place. Smart growth is like a good recipe you perfect over the years. It takes you awhile to find that perfect mix of controlled development and quality of life issues. How do we grow without affecting our beloved farmland and our cherished green spaces? Planning!

Unfortunately a good percentage of small towns do not have regulations in place to be able to control their growth. When a farm goes up for auction, a developer will buy it and subdivide it with houses or commercial buildings. When the next farm goes on the auction block the same thing happens again. And before you know it, an almost new community has been formed. Leaders in these towns need to work now to protect their rich history of farmland and protect against the perils that this "sprawl" can bring upon a community.

And finally, economic diversity is a must if you want to remain vital. Communities must be careful about not putting "all their eggs in one basket." A recent example would be those communities that in the 1980s and 90s, worked hard to lure companies in the auto industry. My community was one of those. These companies have been some of our best corporate citizens over the years and employ more people than any other industry. Now with the global economic struggles these large auto manufacturers are experiencing, communities that were successful in filling their industrial parks with auto suppliers are seeing shutdowns and layoffs, and are experiencing unemployment rates they have not seen in twenty years. We mourn these losses because these companies have been part of our communities' family.

Diversify your mix of business. It's a town's best road to economic success.

If you have ever taken a trip across your state, I am sure that you are very aware that not every small town is lined with big trees, homes with picket fences and people who sit on their front porches and drink lemonade. As I admitted before, there are small towns in America that do have their share of serious problems and some are terminally ill.

You can't talk about small towns and not talk about the rural communities that are barely surviving today. There is nothing sexy about poverty, poor health and the uneducated. What is appealing, however, is the number of organizations out there fighting for rural America and its people.

Al Cross says it's no secret that rural communities are the heart of this great country. As director for the Institute for Rural Journalism and Community Issues based at the University of Kentucky in Lexington, he says for many of us, they are highly desirable and valued places to live. Cross says, "It's no secret that rural America has been under siege. We must learn from these bitter lessons and shift our focus away from just industrial recruitment as ways and means of survival and move toward home grown entrepreneurship. We must give the heart of America a new beat."

Dee Davis couldn't agree more. Davis is what you could call an activist of rural community issues. As president of the Center for Rural Strategies in the small town of Whitesburg, Kentucky (Pop. 1,600), he and his group work to create campaigns and build coalitions around rural policy issues. When they organized, they wanted to be able to tell a different story about small town and country living.

"We saw during our visits to rural areas all across the country that folks in small towns were very engaged, working tirelessly, coaching little league, sitting on the school boards, volunteering for community activities," Davis says. "However, because of this multi-tasking, their communities were falling further behind. They kept blaming themselves, 'If I could only work harder.' What was happening was that they were so involved with what they had going on, they were unconnected with the world outside their own communities."

One major goal of the center, is to reconnect them with the world outside their own, to start a narrative and let them know, they do not have to "go it alone."

Despite how hard we try, rural Americans may never get away from the stereotype of television shows like *The Beverly Hillbillies*. For years, people watched that show and they got it in their minds that is what happens in the hills of rural America. It's hard to deprogram this thinking after watching 274 episodes for more than forty-five years.

Don't get me wrong. I loved this show, and laughed with the rest of the country when watching it. However, like many television programs sometimes do, it has caused people to develop negative perceptions of those who live in rural America, including that of being totally isolated and decades behind the rest of the country.

This leads me into an interesting story about one of the victories of the Center for Rural Strategies. This victory made them legendary when they went up against the corporate world of national television and won. It all had to do with the proposed new television reality show that CBS was planning to produce called the *Real Beverly Hillbillies*.

I remember what I said the moment I read about that, "You have got to be kidding me! Another show just waiting to embarrass rural America."

Why? Why in the world would anyone want to see a family who has never traveled before, be taken out of their familiar surroundings, hoisted into the world of Beverly Hills, and watched and laughed at like as they swim around in a fish bowl? It just didn't make sense.

Davis and all his counterparts were outraged, as were folks all across rural America. School kids started letter writing campaigns and college groups started picketing their local television affiliates.

But nothing changed.

After a massive, national newspaper advertising campaign, funded by groups that felt as strongly as Davis and his group, they actually went to Los Angeles to meet with television executives.

But nothing changed.

Then they had the brilliant idea to picket the Viacom shareholders meeting in New York with all their groups, including members of the United Mine Workers Association.

Finally, something changed.

The network dropped the idea of the television show. Davis swears he thinks the network executives got tired of them and threw their hands up and said "we give."

In an area where challenges are many and victories are few, this win felt good.

The Center continues today to work for those who are unable to speak for themselves and has created an environment for positive change. To keep rural America updated on the issues of the week, the Center started a daily on-line newspaper called the Daily Yonder at www.dailyyonder.com. This source of news and commentary tracks the news and events as well as the issues that are facing those in the rural U.S.

Small towns need to pay specific attention to what they have to offer. Davis says if the statistics are correct, then half the baby boomers plan to move when they retire and half of them want to move to a small town, sometimes back to their own hometown. But for these communities to lure them home, they must become amenity rich and offer the coffee shops, restaurants, and various livability options. "While they are idealizing their youth, they also know they need more than just their heart to move for," Davis insists. Small towns do have an opportunity to lure this group, they just need to pay attention and make themselves more desirable.

*T*he one thing we do in small town America is not kid ourselves. No matter how hard we try, we are never going to be the place for everyone. I have seen people come and I have seen them go. I have seen people move to small town American in hopes of experiencing a new way of life, only to miss the fast-paced world they left behind and move back within a few years. I have seen businesses invest thousands of dollars in order to offer some type of product or service, and within months find that the small town population was not enough to support their business. We hate it when this happens, but we know it is part of life in any size town in America.

We have flaws—but nothing in my opinion that could be considered a deal breaker. All towns, big and small, have their own issues.

So we tend to focus on the positive. Those factors you cannot find in every town in America like low crime rates, affordable cost of living, pharmacies that still deliver prescriptions, and knowing all the kids (and their parents) in your son's third grade class.

So why, you might ask, are some people and companies just not that into small town America?

I will just let you decide for yourself on your next visit here. I suggest you pack a suitcase; you may want to stay for awhile.

SMALL TOWN *Sexy*

is admitting your flaws and accepting the fact

that not everyone is "into" a small town lifestyle.

"The biggest things
happen in the smallest of places."
—Kim Huston, author

SMALL TOWN SEXY:
THE AFTERGLOW

*H*ave you ever found yourself waking up in the morning, just seconds before the reality of the new day sets in, and just wished during the night, a time machine had taken you back to being twelve-years-old again? I do—and quite often. At that age, the most important decisions I had to make in a day were where I would ride my bike and what I would make for lunch.

Except for the birth of my daughters, my childhood days in my small town of Bloomfield are probably the most memorable experiences of my life. Those days were so simple, so innocent, a time where no one talked about "being stressed" and the word "multi-task" was not in our vocabulary.

Cell phones would not have been necessary as my mom always knew where I was, and never worried about me heading off on my bike as I set out on a new adventure on the country back roads. I so often long for these vivid images to come to life again, and I am once again at home, hanging out on the corner with my friends, just deciding which direction to take and what we are going to do.

Nostalgia is a very powerful feeling.

I have not found one universal term for the way people think about their small towns; I have found however, by just talking to people about their childhood and their small hometowns, there is, without a doubt, a smile that comes across their face with every memory. What I have learned is that *Small Town Sexy* means different things to different people depending on the kind of life they have led and the experiences they have had.

Small Town Sexy is:

—Realizing you are a small town addict, and not wanting an intervention.

—Knowing that despite your size, you can still conduct big business.

—Celebrating your heritage for all to see.

—Knowing that the size of your town has no merit to its success.

—About people coming back, and others discovering small towns for the first time.

—Getting involved in the decision making process.

—Enjoying the thrills of your big city neighbors.

—Embracing the unique individuals who make up community and accepting the fact that not everyone is into small town life.

I find myself back to that one essential question, what is *Small Town Sexy*? It now has become quite clear:

First, *Small Town Sexy* is a feeling.

It is that feeling that comes over you when you close your eyes and think about your life there. It's a nurturing calm that for an instant takes you back to a "good place." A place where the air was clean, the sky was blue and was never measured by size but by the quality of life you led.

Second, *Small Town Sexy* is people. Though we are scattered from coast to coast, there is a connection, a kindred spirit if you will, that makes us all part of this wonderful small town society.

Who are the people that make small towns sexy?

We are mothers, fathers, teachers, students, doctors, volunteers, and entrepreneurs. We are rich snobs and we are rednecks. We have GEDs and MBAs, we are retired and on unemployment.

We live downtown, on farms, in mobile homes, and sometimes at the end of dirt roads.

We drive cars, trucks, hybrids and four-wheelers and we have been known to drive a tractor to our senior prom.

We have old money, new money and some of us have no money at all.

We are all the people of *Small Town Sexy*.

Small towns are some of the most inviting places you will ever go.

They are places where people still ride bikes, and not because it's the "green" thing to do, but because it allows you to see things that can't be seen from the windows of cars.

Small towns are where the smell of freshly mowed grass lingers for what seems like blocks, and where people know your name in the local hardware stores, and all you have to do to pay is say "charge it."

In small towns you will find old signs still painted on the sides of barns, stores that close at five o'clock and a church on every corner.

A small town is like a favorite song playing on the radio. You just can't get it off your mind no matter how hard you try. They are not ritzy or glitzy, but are simple and genuine just like the people who live there. They are small in size, but enormous in spirit and are always alive and full of personality.

Can you live a happy, SEXY life in a small town?

You can live a happy, sexy life in any town. I don't think the size of the community you live in is going to determine whether you are happy or not. There are too many other factors that will do that for you.

Are you in a happy relationship?

Are you financially stable?

Are you healthy?

Those things get you up in the morning and help you sleep at night.

Not particularly the town you are waking up in. But, loving where you live and the environment that surrounds you every day, has everything to do with your peace of mind.

Let's face it; chances are many of you will never move to a small town. That's absolutely no problem—we understand and we love you anyway.

If you don't plan to live in small town America, let me encourage you to do the next best thing. Step away from the computer, turn off your TV, get out of your office and get away. Get away to the amazing "Byways of America" and experience the wonderful world of small towns. Life happens fast. Don't let it pass you by.

Do I ever wonder, what if? What if I got a "do-over" and had the chance to change my decision about coming home to small town America after college? I wouldn't be honest if I said it doesn't cross my mind on occasion, but I have never regretted that decision, not once. Especially, when I look out my "window to the world" and see this truly unbelievable slice of heaven looking back at me. My days in small town America would not be complete without scenes I see each day out of my window, including the shopkeepers preparing for another day of business, the stay-at-home moms talking as fast as they're walking, and those wonderful men, hurrying into the local diner for a morning of local news with their coffee.

I know that my life at age twelve is gone and my memories are all that I have of those good times. Because today, in reality, the buildings seem smaller, the Tobacco Festival is gone, and there is a whole new set of girls standing on that infamous corner watching the cars go by just waiting for the moment when they are old enough to leave. And if they are lucky, and the passion in them is as strong as mine, they, too, will find their way back to small town America just as I did.

I am not sure I have lived my best life yet, because I have a lot of life worth living, but what I am sure about, is that the life I look forward to living will be in small town America.

And that, my friend, is *Small Town Sexy*.

appendix

SMALL TOWN SEXY STORIES

*I*t has been a pleasure being able to share with you some of my childhood stories throughout this book. I hope they have inspired some memories of your own and allowed you to reminisce about times gone by.

During this writing journey, I heard from many good friends, some who grew up in small towns and now live the big city life and others who, after living a big city life have found their paradise in small town America.

I have included their stories to entertain you about a simpler life in a simpler place.

Please enjoy!

MARK GREEN, LEXINGTON, KENTUCKY

*G*rowing up in a small town definitely made me who I am. Most of my youth, from age eight through high school, was spent in Lebanon, Kentucky, population then roughly 5,000. The economy was built on tobacco farming. I walked three blocks to grade school, five blocks to junior high. We lived three blocks from downtown, which was only five or six square blocks but was jammed with so many thriving small businesses that it seemed to have many, many distinct little microcosms for the passing pedestrian to experience. It was largely a foot-traffic and slow-moving-vehicle zone. We hadn't retreated behind locked doors and into our rooms where each of us had our own telephone, television, computer, game system, etc. In town, storefronts engaged the passing foot and vehicle traffic. Experts claim more than ninety percent of communication is non-verbal. We had eye contact with one another. It produced a deeper connection and knowledge of our fellow townsmen. Even if that interaction was very occasional.

Because Lebanon was a farm town, there was sometimes a Dr. Seuss, Whoville-ish quality when the unique folks who spend almost all their time on the farm came into town for special events with an excited gleam in their eye. Lebanon was a tobacco farming town—that's mostly gone now. There were at least three major warehouses where the farmers would bring their crop in the late winter at auction time. There was a special smell and feel and energy in the warehouses at auction time. This was when many local families made their big paycheck for the year. There was even an energy present in a truckload—or sometimes a wagonload cruising by on Main Street behind a tractor—of the product passing by on the road on its way to the warehouse. It was a labor-intensive hand-worked product. It was personal industry and accomplishment on parade. And it was about to be converted into the dollars that were going to flow through the local economy to every merchant, service provider and church in the community.

Lebanon was/is a multidenominational Christian place, but the largest denomination was Catholic. The Catholic church, its rectory, parish hall and school stand nearest the center of town. Another half dozen parishes dot the county. Besides all the ritual and structure and tradition that come with Catholicism, perhaps the biggest characteristic that it brings made Lebanon and Marion County unique in small-town central Kentucky: tolerance for alcohol! Why, it was even sold retail. It was so tolerated that the liquor stores had drive-up windows so that a motorist, who might not be a local, could purchase beer and liquor without having to fully face the world in doing so. Even if they were not the legal age of twenty-one. But that transaction could be a nerve-wracking one for a teen. The window sales clerk might be merry and mirthful, but other times he possessed the probing eyes of bird of prey, inspecting the would-be buyer carefully for some mysterious quality that rendered him or her worthy of conducting a transaction. Sometimes there were a few questions. Who are you? Who is your family? Where do you live—the part of town or the county, not your specific address.

Drinking and driving was almost invariably about to happen so the interaction between the windows of the vehicle and the building involved some assessment that the buyer's background indicated that they could handle their alcohol, was not an agent of a non-home team law enforcement agency, or the offspring of someone who would vigorously object to what was about to transpire.

Apparently this local social contract was almost unique in the state. And it was irresistibly attractive to the youth of the region. Two local nightclubs were the largest in the state for several decades until the late 1970s. A small local black club was on the "chitlin circuit" and hosted many of the top performers of the '50s and '60s who weren't welcome in segregated establishments. The top bands in the state performed in my hometown on weekends regularly, and it attracted hundreds and sometimes a few thousand of out-of-town residents looking for fun times on Friday and Saturday night.

I was part of a large extended family since my mother was one of thirteen children who'd grow up on one of the farms outside of Lebanon. There were literally fifty first cousins, and virtually everyone managed to gather for holidays or the yearly reunion as I was growing up and until I went to college. It was a Catholic family, of course. It was an amazing, loving experience.

I like people. I like meeting new people. I enjoy crowds.

This is just a small sampling of what the small town I grew up in was like, but clearly it is an important part of who I am today.

Float Fever by Sammy Beam, Hollywood, California

*I*t's a typical Monday evening for me. I've packed the truck with everything I'll be needing for my next three days in Santa Barbara. I make one final walk-through to see that my house in the heart of old, slightly seedy, but up-and-coming Hollywood is secure.

I am what's known as a decorative artist. I design and hand paint elaborate, Northern European-inspired ceiling and wall treatments for the super wealthy who want the very best and can afford to get it. I'm an interior designer these days, though, and I've landed a plum gig in Santa Barbara's Hope Ranch estates. Its land is the most expensive and impressive real estate in the nation, outside of Manhattan.

I'd been painting my client's seaside mansion there for two years when she approached me with an offer. She'd fired her designer a few months back and was left with this beautifully painted showplace that was still practically empty. She wanted me to have contracts drawn up, to come on board as the designer, and to get the place furnished and finished. As it turns out, I have a gift for it. Each week I spend three days in my office or the showrooms, and two days on site. At this point, I've schlepped up and down the 101 so many times that I tend to ignore the mountain and ocean views completely. I don't really see any of the beauty that Southern California has to offer because I'm usually lost in thought. On many days, when there's nothing too pressing and the music's just right, I slip into daydreams of my home town: What it would be like if I hadn't left it behind, and what it might be like if I ever returned to it. While I don't realistically envision myself ever making a home there again, it's fun to dream about.

Most small towns across America have something to be proud of ... something that sets them apart. Once a year, these villages haul that "something" out and parade it around in celebration. Our home town's claim to fame was tobacco. Our farmers grew it, our parents smoked it, and some of our locals chewed it, right off the twist. Our home town was a mecca of burley tobacco warehouses where it was collected and auctioned to dealers who came in from all points east, west, north, and south. Hence, the Bloomfield Tobacco Festival.

As small children, we were regaled by tales of Tobacco Festivals past. We were shown photographs and home movies of parades long gone by, and we wondered why they'd stopped holding these events. They had been big deals, HUGE DEALS, in the fifties. In those days there were pageants that drew contestants from all over the state. These contestants were all vying for positions in the Royal Tobacco Festival Court. The King, Queen, Prince, and Princess were judged on things like beauty and personal sparkle. My older sister Tonni was crowned Princess in 1955, and we have the photograph of her, a Prince named Freddy, and an unknown King and Queen, (from Shelbyville) to prove it. Of course the very first Tobacco Festival Queen, and the only one anybody truly remembers, was Geraldine.

I don't think that there was one child in our little town who didn't have an enormous crush on Geraldine. She was the closest thing to a real live movie star that there ever was in Bloomfield . . . tall and shapely with wavy auburn hair that fell, like satin ribbons, across caramel-colored shoulders, impeccably-proportioned bone structure, and eyes that glowed like ice-blue lanterns. Even more important was her spirit. She was funny and fiery, hard-working, smart as a whip, and good to have on your side when the chips were down. These are just a few reasons why Geraldine was the Tobacco Festival Queen to end them all. But I digress.

In 1969 it was decided to bring back the festival, to see if it worked, and to hold it, thereafter, once every five years or so. The pageant was reduced to the crowning of a festival Queen. That was okay. Nobody seemed to mind. After all, there would still be a parade. There would be floats, horses, marching bands, and a bicycle-decorating contest. That's right. Any kid with a bike and a couple of skeins of crepe paper could parade down the main drag and show off his or her decorative genius.

I knew, the minute my Momma asked what theme I was considering for my entry, that I was in trouble. After all, she was the creative one in the family. I knew that she was only asking my opinion so that the floor would be open to HER opinion. So it was a done deal. Senseless or not, I was going to be dressed as Santa Claus on a Christmas-themed bicycle, surrounded by the pumpkins and Indian corn of a brown and orange Saturday morning in mid-October.

"Everybody loves Christmas," Momma said, "It's the most popular season of the year! You're sure to win." And, with that statement, I was relieved of any creative responsibility whatsoever.

My bike wouldn't do. It was a sporty, mini Western Flyer, super hot, but low to the ground. It's training wheels had been removed years before, but I hadn't yet graduated to a full-sized one, like my sister's, with a banana seat and elongated handle bars.

"No biggie. You'll learn to ride your sister's. We'll never be able to make any kind of statement with that little thing."

"But it's a GIRL'S BIKE," I protested.

"Well, after we're finished with it, nobody'll notice a silly thing like that."

Momma was right. It was no big deal. I'd ridden my sister's bike dozens of times. It was no big deal at all . . . until Momma had Daddy attach the heavy metal rods that would support the enormous "MERRY CHRISTMAS" banner to the handle bars. They made the contraption top-heavy and sensitive to even the slightest breeze. Every day, after school, it was practice, practice, practice. I was having trouble trying to maneuver what had become a high-profile death mobile. I was just starting to catch on when the bar was raised, yet again. Now I'd have to try it with a cumbersome bag of pointy, old-fashioned toys strapped to my back. Then came the cotton-covered buckram beard that would obstruct my breathing and constrict any facial movement. Fun, fun, fun!

On the Friday night prior to the parade it was decided. I'd done the best that I could do, but there was still a chance of my toppling, mid-route, creating a pile up, and bringing the parade to a screeching halt. Daddy would have to walk along to steady me if things got bad.

The next morning, Daddy and I climbed Fairfield hill on foot. I was dressed as Santa, and pushing the 900-pound death mobile. Daddy looked like a Secret Service agent in his tweed suit, top coat, and jaunty dress hat. Not a word was spoken until everyone was lined up and ready for take off.

"Son, you think you got it?" I honestly didn't know the answer.

After about fifty feet of coasting, I got it. It was just a matter of handle bars and brakes. I didn't look at Daddy, even once, as we proceeded along the parade route, but I knew he was there if something were to go wrong. It didn't.

Did I win the contest? No. It turns out that Christmas was not the most popular season at the Bloomfield Tobacco Festival that year. The winners were the Howard brothers, on bikes that had been tricked out to resemble John Deere tractors. It was a brilliant and appropriate miracle of illusion, accomplished with only a few cardboard boxes. To this day, I will never figure out how they did it. Of course, their parents had done all of the work for them, but who was I to talk?

In the mid-seventies, a new breed of local officials got the itch and decided to bring back the festival, full throttle, and to make it an annual three-day event. The Queen would be chosen by the spin of a wheel, making it far less glamorous but far more politically correct. This meant that even the most humble chairwoman would have a chance at wearing that tiara. Many did.

By this time, we were in our early teens and students at Bloomfield Junior High School, or good old BJHS. It sat, like a story book castle, on a steep hill that loomed over the town as a reminder of our educational responsibilities. Every afternoon, at the sound of the final bell, we town kids were freed. We'd zip past the long lines of farm kids and country kids as they were slowly herded onto their buses. Many of them had over an hour's ride until they were dropped at the end of their often mile-long driveways. We town kids, though, were FREE! We'd escape through any accessible exit and scramble down the craggy hillside, in groups of two or three, and begin our short journeys home, with many stops along the way.

A few of these afternoons were more exalted, and caused a more jubilant exodus than others: The last day before Christmas break, the last day before summer vacation, and, most special of all, the Friday that kicked off the Bloomfield Tobacco Festival! The air was thick with the electricity of the first autumnal nip. You could hear the music from the carnival rides that had been set up along Depot Street. You could smell the cotton candy before you'd even stepped a foot off school property. This was small town nirvana.

There was a group of us town boys who stuck together like glue. My best friend Lonnie was three years older than the rest of us, which meant that he demanded automatic respect. He was a little nerdy, but crafty and funny, so he was the ring leader. He and I had joined the local Historical Society and, by 1976, had formed an off-shoot of that group made up of younger members. It was more a social scene, with brief glimpses of history, than anything else. We'd meet at any public venue that could be hoodwinked into thinking that we were on the up and up. We got a few of the prettier local girls interested, and that was all it took. It was on. We were a force to be reckoned with.

More than history, we were interested in activities and projects that made us seem more adult. We wanted a say in things but we weren't quite sure what those things were. We'd meet once a week to decide what we were going to do. The Tobacco Festival of 1976 was an answer to our prayers. We would build ourselves a float, and we would enter the parade contest, which, of course, we would win.

The theme of the parade that year was "Old Kentucky Romances," so what old Kentucky romance would our float represent? It took us three seconds to come to a decision with no voting at all. The Romantic Tragedy, the historic tale of Jereboam and Anna Beauchamp. The couple had died as punishment for a very romantic crime and been buried, in each others' arms, in our local cemetery in 1826. It had everything: Passion, glamor, and death. It was Southern Gothic, pure and simple.

The story went something like this. Anna Beauchamp was the mistress of a Frankfort big wig, one Col. Solomon Sharp. He knocked her up, and then dismissed her, leaving her in disgrace. Making matters worse, the kid was stillborn. A while later, there came a sexy young lawyer named Jereboam Beauchamp. He fell for Anna. He fell hard. He asked her to marry him and she said she would but on one condition. He would have to avenge Colonel Sharp's slight by murdering the old coot. Jereboam considered her request and he thought, Okay . . . How difficult could it be?

So Jereboam snuck up to an alley-facing door of Solomon Sharp's mansion in Frankfort. He'd disguised himself as an African-American servant with a black cloth over his face. He knocked on the door. When Sharp opened it, Jereboam knifed him good. That's when Jereboam got stupid. He lifted the cloth, exposing his identity. He just HAD to explain, to Sharp, exactly why he was being offed. Just then, Sharp's wife rushed in to see what was causing all of the ruckus, and there stood Jereboam Beauchamp. EXPOSED!

He hightailed it to Anna's and they went on the lam, but they didn't get far. They were caught in no time flat. Anna, feeling bad for all the trouble she'd caused, refused to leave Jereboam's side. She insisted on being imprisoned with him and, because they were newlyweds, the jailer obliged. Anna was a tough cookie. She had a plan. She'd smuggled some contraband, a small knife and a vial of poison, into their cell. First, she wrote a nice, rambling poem for their epitaph. Then she and Jereboam drank the poison, but all it did was make them feel lousy. She pulled out the knife. It worked on Anna and she passed quickly. Jereboam lived on, wounded and pissed, to be hanged the following day. They were buried in the same coffin in our local cemetery and, as far as we kids were concerned, that made their story ours to do with as we pleased.

We decided that the float should be red and black. Those colors were readily available in the crepe paper section of Snider's Drug Store. It would need some gallows and a nice, proper noose. That part was no problem. My Daddy had taught me to tie a noose when I was eight-years-old. Our school principal let us borrow a set of portable stairs from the gym, and we borrowed a big wooden box, for the platform of the gallows, from my brother in law. The tobacco wagon, upon which all of this would be assembled, was Lonnie's dad's. It would be up to Timmy and Billy to build the most important element, a really spooky coffin. They automatically knew that the best place to find the free lumber that they needed was Buzzard's Roost.

Buzzard's Roost was our town's obligatory Haunted Mansion. It stood just a few lots down from the warehouse where we were building the float. It had been a showplace in its prime but, like a house built upon the sands, it had shifted and crumbled from that day on. Its last inhabitants, in the early sixties, had been low-end renters in rooms to let. Many of them had left lock, stock, and barrel behind when they moved on. It was a great place to loot when materials were needed. You had to be careful though. Buzzards Roost was rumored to be the clandestine trysting place for local drunks with homosexual proclivities. HORRORS! We always made plenty of noise, to frighten off deviants, when entering Buzzard's Roost.

Timmy and Billy set out for coffin lumber and, in no time flat, we heard their victory cries as they made their way back up Fairfield Hill. They didn't have lumber. They didn't need lumber anymore. They had the actual goods... The creepiest coffin that ever existed! In truth, it was an just old wooden banana crate that someone, decades before, had padded and upholstered, and turned into a cheapjack, homemade divan. Its disintegrated covering, gray and gauzy, sent out ghostly tendrils that floated and danced with every step the boys took. It was the final jewel in our crown.

On the morning of the parade, we all rose early to find dim skies and a premature freeze. Onward and upward, we gathered at the starting point. It took only minutes for the judges to declare us First Place, Non-Commercial winners, and off we went.

The second that our creation bounced and rumbled out of the warehouse, the sleet began sifting down. Nothing, however, could stop true success for the wickedly deserving. Becky, portraying our Anna, lay, white as a sheet and motionless, as freezing rain pelted her pallid cheeks. She didn't flinch. She didn't breathe. I, as the hangman, led Jereboam up the stairs to his fate. Most of the spectators gathered that day had no clue as to what we were trying to represent with that float. Its gruesome elements, though, were a novel diversion from the hay bales and cast-iron garden furniture that usually adorned parade entries. The crowd went wild.

In the downpour, it didn't take long for all of the parade floats to wilt. Queen candidates and local beauties shivered, in their mothers' fake fur stoles, as their lacquered hairdos wept. The mittened children of business owners did their best to look jolly as they fumbled attempts to toss butterscotch candies to the undaunted crowd. The pastel dyes of multicolored tissue and crepe paper bled and pooled, like iridescent oil slicks, on the blacktop. Twenty-eight floats died a slow death that day. Ours, the twenty-ninth, blossomed and came to life in the face of adversity. The red and black of its crepe paper mingled and oozed into a delightfully ghastly pallor. By the time we'd reached the stoplight, our entry had morphed into a runny, congealed confection of ghoulish delight.

After that, I was hooked. I had Float Fever. Each year, I'd start planning and gathering in early September. If I didn't have a sponsor, (our history group had disbanded when skating parties became a more attractive option,) I'd find one. Every year, the floats became bigger and bigger productions. By the time I was in the eleventh grade, my teachers knew that I probably wouldn't be absorbing much knowledge or completing an assignment until after the Tobacco Festival. I was just too focused. There would be time enough for education AFTER the important stuff.

Parade themes came and went. I always found a way to tie in a beloved old time Hollywood blockbuster, and take home the trophy. By the time the festival committee came up with "The Sound of Music," I'd graduated from high school. I was a freshman in college, I was far away from home, and I was miserable. I hated the university. I hadn't wanted to go. I didn't want to leave my home town because I'd never even fantasized about a life anywhere but there. Even worse, I couldn't stand the thought of attending the Tobacco Festival as an observer. I had to find a way to participate. I didn't look for long. An offer came my way.

The president of the senior class of my alma mater contacted me. They were at a loss, and couldn't come up with an idea for their float entry. They wanted something spectacular, and they were willing to do the work, but they needed direction. I threw them the idea of Gershwin's *An American in Paris*. They loved it. We were, once again, on.

We worked, over the phone, for a couple of weeks. I gave orders.

They were followed. The week before the parade, I got a call begging me to be there in person. My directions were being lost in translation. I was elated. I lied and begged off from school. My parents understood my needs, and went along with it. I spent those last days before the festival, hands on, at the warehouse.

The entry was to be a sort of parade within a parade. There would be banner girls, in cancan skirts and bonnets, leading the way. Flower peddlers, street walkers, and Parisienne sophisticates, with live poodles, would orbit the structure during lulls in the procession. The body of the float represented the city of Paris itself, with street lights and a panoramic view of the Eiffel Tower as a backdrop. That's where the stars of the show, the two young lovers, stood amidst balloons and slick-haired, spit-curled fashion models draped in bias-cut black satin and waving enormous silver feather fans. Simple. To the point.

On the night before the parade, when all of the final touches were being applied, I was approached by the parade chairperson and the chairman of the festival. They needed to have a word with me.

"We have a little bit of a problem, and we're wondering if you can help us out. There have been complaints . . . complaints about you. Parents of the other kids, whose groups are competing tomorrow, have a problem with you. Churches, too. They've come to us saying that it isn't fair that you're working on this float. They say that there's not a chance in hell of anyone else winning non-commercial as long as you're in the running. Let's face it, your work is on a professional level."

I tried to talk them down, but they would have none of it. They tried another approach. They claimed that, since I wasn't a member of the senior class, I had no right to contribute. My counterclaim was that, as in every past parade, most of the floats were being tricked out by mothers and most of the students were just standing around under their direction. It went nowhere. They wanted me out.

"Maybe, instead of kicking me out for being too good," I argued, "THEY SHOULD GET BETTER! This is ridiculous! I am NOT a professional! I am only SEVENTEEN-YEARS-OLD!" That's when the young parade chairperson got hot.

"BIG DEAL! I'm only twenty-one and I'm in charge of the WHOLE PARADE! Got that? You need to listen to what I'm telling you. You should move on. There are people who build floats, who make it their careers, in New York. That's what you should do. You need to get yourself to New York and LEAVE MY PARADE ALONE!" By this time, there was a crowd gathering.

"And if I don't?" I was chin to chin with her and we were both shaking. The festival chairman was seething. The two of them got silent, exchanged a look, and they lowered the boom.

"You can put down that staple gun, this minute, and you can walk away. We'll drop the whole thing and forget it ever happened. However, if we should find out that you had anything more to do with this float, that you even made so much as a phone call to anyone who's working on it, it's over. Disqualified." As I retreated, I turned to lock tear-filled eyes with the senior class president, but I was cut off by the wagging finger of the parade chairperson. "NOT A WORD!"

It had been my moment of painful truth. I'd been handed what I considered a pink slip from the entire town. The only thing I had to offer had been rejected. The blow was softened, only a little, by a late night phone call. The class officials had held a meeting and decided that it was better to be disqualified than to be embarrassed. They couldn't pull it off without me.

We all gathered, once more, in the wee, gray hours that were left. We worked in vengeful, anger-driven silence, and we completed our task. The float was glorious. It was a multicolored marvel that stood out, among the others, and shone like the top of the Chrysler Building. It was my last hurrah and my final goodbye to a town that would soon become only a place that I would visit. These days I visit it, in person, only once a year. I visit it daily, though, in all of my dreams.

BETTY SAYERS, HOLDREGE, NEBRASKA
www.nebraskaruralliving.com

*S*mall towns are sexy places to live . . . if by "sexy" you mean a wide variety of people shot like colorful silk threads through hundreds of daily crossings and conversations, time and space to express and explore a talent or a passion, the richness and balance one experiences living day to day in neighborhoods that house 3 generations.

We eat fresh, locally grown, and often organically grown food. We appreciate good food and some of us actually do cook because a 10 minute commute makes home life a potential for most families. For exercise enthusiasts, small towns are the place to be. Destination walkers like myself easily step 5,000 times in a day, and the marathon trainers, bicyclists and joggers set out on any street and go east, west, north, or south to face the breeze or see the sunrise or sunset as they please.

ALL–BARDSTOWN / ALL–AMERICAN BY NED JOHNSON, TAMPA, FLORIDA

"*N*ed!"
                Several minutes pass, but the young boy continues to shoot baskets on the outdoor goal, hanging loosely on the garage door above the gravel driveway.

"Ned . . . come on in . . . time for dinner!"

The boy imagines he's Louie Dampier and nails a shot to the screams of the Kentucky Wildcat fans.

"EDWARD BELL JOHNSON, JR.! Come in now!"

OK, She's serious now—the full name was used. Time to get inside. He places the ball down on the gravel driveway in front of the garage, knowing it will be there upon his return. Besides, if the basketball is out, maybe Donald Ray Jenkins or Mike Motley will come across the street and play, giving him an excuse to come back out.

The young boy runs into the house where the All-Bardstown/All-American family awaits: Dad in his police uniform, getting a hot, home-cooked meal before going on the night shift; Brother Charlie just home from basketball practice at St. Joe Prep, his white shirt and blazer laying on the nearby ironing board for Mom to press; Sister Jane is absent, as she stayed behind in New Haven to complete her senior year at St. Catharine—she's the valedictorian of the class and staying with Papaw and Granny Jane; and Mom, perfect makeup and dress, always the class of the family.

Dinner conversation starts with Charlie's day, then mine. Mom and Dad are always interested in our lives, and most of the time already know what we did but like hearing it from us.

Then the talk moves to the Ballard family . . . Mom talks about Bert stopping by earlier to fix her dryer. "I called him at 9:00 and he was here by 10 . . . he's one of my five perfect brothers, you know."

How many times have we heard about the five perfect brothers? It's still fun to hear the love Mom has for each of them: Bert, Jerry, Hamburger, Bobby and Leon. Who is her favorite? All of them.

Oh my gosh, it's Jane! My sister shows up—she got a ride to Bardstown. Everybody hugs everybody because it's been forever since we've seen her . . . yesterday.

There's laughter and carrying on in the Johnson Family tradition throughout the remainder of the meal. Now it's time for dishes. This should be a chore, but Mom always makes it fun.

"What do you want to play tonight? Concentration, Password, Jeopardy?"

We pick a game and play it with competitive spirit. I wash, Jane dries and Charlie stacks—a total team effort while Mom runs the game. Dad moves to the living room to watch either *The Huntley/Brinkley Report* or the *CBS Evening News*.

After dinner, because there's just a bit of light out, Charlie takes me into the backyard to play whiffle ball. He pitches and I hit. We play the Reds vs. the Dodgers. I have to bat in the style of whoever is up: I crouch as Pete Rose; I bunt as Maury Wills. When Charlie imitates Don Drysdale, I know to duck because the first pitch is coming straight at me.

How lucky can a kid be that a brother who is eight years older makes time every night to play?

The spirited game ends when I hit the ball in Mom's prize rosebushes a third time. She announces, "Time to come in."

Dad is leaving. They share a kiss and an "I love you," and we promise Dad to mind Mom. We go into the house and do homework. Mom seems to always know, somehow, what homework needs to be done. If I didn't know better, I'd swear she actually talked to the nuns at St. Joe Elementary and the brothers at St. Joe Prep. Jane, of course, completed hers—she's a saint who is most difficult for Charlie and I to follow.

After homework is done, we watch a couple of comedies on TV. We only get two channels: NBC and CBS. Sometimes, when the conditions are right, we can turn the UHF button to the "32" and get ABC—sometimes not.

At 9:00, Mom tells me it's time for bed, so after my usual protest, it's off to my room. She knows I'm not going to sleep right away, because I'll be playing my Strat-O-Matic baseball game under the covers, using a flashlight. I play for an hour until she calls out.

The gig is up, so I put the game away and go to sleep.

The next day, it will all start again.

Such was the life of the All-Bardstown/All-American family. Looking back, we didn't have much money, didn't have much technology, didn't have much in the way of material possessions. But we were the cliché: a loving family who thought they were rich in every way because of doting parents, caring siblings, and above all, lots and lots of laughter.

I might not have been Opie Taylor (although when we lived in New Haven, dad was Town Marshal); I might not have been Beaver Cleaver (although mom was always meticulously dressed and Charlie had a friend she called Eddie Haskell); but I'll match my childhood with anyone who has ever lived on the basis of love, caring, and laughter.

I am Ned, er, EDWARD BELL JOHNSON, JR. I am a lucky boy from Smalltown, U.S.A.

KAREN KELLING, WESTCLIFFE, COLORADO

*T*he old adage of "pictures don't do it justice" rings true in Westcliffe, Colorado.

You need to experience the millions of stars twinkling above you on a clear cloudless night.

You need to listen to the quaking Aspens in the fall.

You need to be in awe as a 100-head count of elk rush in front of your car and scatter up into the nearby hills, and

You need to watch the mountains as the light of day changes from reds to pinks of sunrise to purples and gold at sunset.

The beauty of nature is all around this area and after ten years, I have yet to enjoy it all. It is an endless nature park in my backyard.

*W*e all have a special small town story in us, and I welcome you to share yours with me. Please visit my website at www.SmallTownSexy.com and post a Blog and share your story with me and other small town enthusiasts across the country.

*T*he population figures in this book are based on the 2000 and estimated 2007 population figures of U.S. Census unless otherwise noted. www.census.gov

Crampton, Norman. *The 100 Best Small Towns in America*. (New York: Arco Publishing, second edition, 1996)

Christensen, Julia. *Big Box Reuse*. (Boston: The MIT Press, 2008)

Schultz, Jack. *Boomtown USA: The 7-1/2 Keys to Big Success Small Towns*. (National Association of Industrial and Office, 2004)

Schultz, Patricia. *1,000 Places to See before you Die*. (New York: Workman Publishing Company, 2003)

Sweitzer, Gerald and Kathy M. Fields. *50 Best Small Southern Towns*. (Atlanta: Peachtree Publishers, second edition, 2007)

Ryan, Rebecca. *Live First, Work Second*. (Madison, WI: Next Generation Consulting, 2007)

Madison, Indiana .... www.visitmadison.org
National Park Service .... www.nps.gov
National Scenic Byway Program .... www.byways.org
Nebraska Rural Living .... www.nebraskaruralliving.com
Next Generation Consulting ....www.nextgenerationconsulting.com
Oberlin, Ohio... www.cityofoberlin.com
Oberlin College .... www.new.oberlin.edu
Springfield, Kentucky.. www.springfieldky.org
St. Catharine College.. www.sccky.edu
Telluride, Colorado.. www.telluridechamber.com
Thomasville, Georgia .... www.thomasvillechamber.com
University of Kentucky .... www.uky.edu
Westcliffe, Colorado .... www.westcliffe-colorado.com
Where to Retire Magazine..www.wheretoretire.com

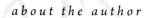

*Y*ou will be hard-pressed to find a person who has more passion about small town America than *Small Town Sexy* author Kim Huston. Born and raised in Bloomfield, Kentucky (Pop. 900), Huston now lives in Bardstown, Kentucky (Pop. 11,000), a small town recognized nationally as one of the best small towns in America. Kim is proud to boast that Bardstown has been mentioned in publications including *50 Best Southern Towns, BoomTown USA, 100 Best Small Towns in America*, was named by *National Geographic Adventure Magazine* as "One of the Next Great Adventure Towns" and was listed by *Where to Retire* Magazine as one of the "Best Places to Retire."

A former broadcast journalist, Kim Huston is now the President of the Nelson County Economic Development Agency in Bardstown, where she and her team oversee all economic development activities including the Chamber of Commerce, Tourism Commission, Industrial Development and Main Street Development.

During her broadcast journalism years, Kim won several Associated Press awards for her feature stories based on events in her hometown and hosted the television program *On Location* that featured the places, events and characters in her county. As an economic recruiter, Kim has the opportunity to talk with companies and site consultants from all across the U.S. about why they choose certain locations and what makes a small town a good place to do big business.

Kim also serves on the Kentucky Association for Economic Development Board of Directors where she has been named the "Economic Development Professional of the Year." She also serves on the Kentucky Workforce Investment Board, chairs the Lincoln Workforce Investment Board and co-chairs a twenty-six county WIRED 65 Initiative that is designed to promote regionalism and bringing big cities together with smaller communities in an effort to work together to become a more competitive region.

Kim is the proud mother of two daughters Erin and Meg. She and her fiancé Mike divide their time between their home in Bardstown and their cabin on the lake.

LaVergne, TN USA
18 March 2010
176439LV00003B/2/P